Anyone *Can* Sew

Anyone *Can* Sew

A STEP-BY-STEP GUIDE TO ESSENTIAL SEWING SKILLS

CHARLOTTE GERLINGS

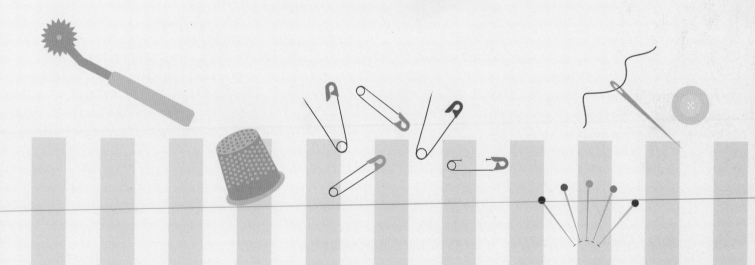

ARCTURUS

This edition published in 2014 by Arcturus Publishing Limited
26/27 Bickels Yard, 151–153 Bermondsey Street,
London SE1 3HA

Copyright © Arcturus Holdings Limited
With grateful acknowledgement to Martha Preston, author of Craft
Workbooks Quilting and Appliqué

ISBN: 978-1-78212-866-3
AD003901UK

Printed in China

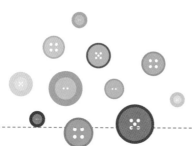

CONTENTS

EQUIPMENT

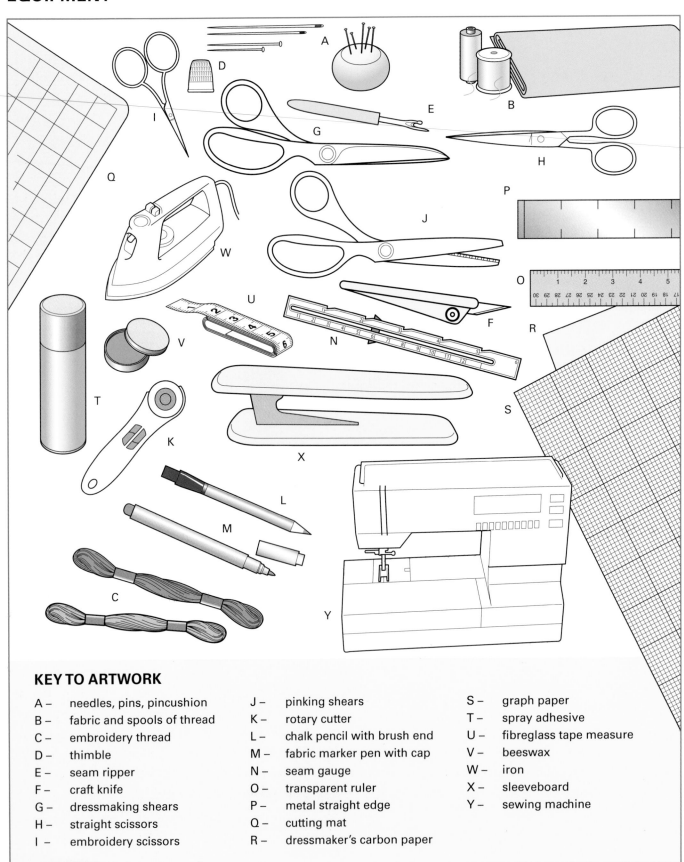

KEY TO ARTWORK

A – needles, pins, pincushion
B – fabric and spools of thread
C – embroidery thread
D – thimble
E – seam ripper
F – craft knife
G – dressmaking shears
H – straight scissors
I – embroidery scissors

J – pinking shears
K – rotary cutter
L – chalk pencil with brush end
M – fabric marker pen with cap
N – seam gauge
O – transparent ruler
P – metal straight edge
Q – cutting mat
R – dressmaker's carbon paper

S – graph paper
T – spray adhesive
U – fibreglass tape measure
V – beeswax
W – iron
X – sleeveboard
Y – sewing machine

INTRODUCTION

Our pre-historic ancestors polished splinters of cattlebone to form the first needles about 35000 years ago and used them to join animal skins together with lengths of sinew. Between then and now, people have sewn clothes for warmth, tents for shelter, sails for voyages of exploration, and flags for nations. It could be argued that a needle and thread in a skilled pair of hands has played as great a part in civilization as the invention of the wheel.

The know-how and ideas contained in this book are aimed at every level of ability, whether you are just starting out or already an experienced needleworker. It is packed with step-by-step instructions in essential sewing skills, from threading a sewing machine to setting a zip fastener or decoding a paper pattern.

And there are over thirty illustrated projects for you to engage with, from hand-stitched glove puppets to machining fully lined curtains; from padded coathangers to making a pair of bedroom slippers or tailoring a smart skirt. There are instructions too for a wide range of bags – totes to clutch bags, peg bags to party favours. If you fancy venturing beyond straight stitching, you can experiment with introductions to patchwork, appliqué or embroidery.

Anyone Can Sew also features what you need in the way of needlework equipment and materials, including the choice of sewing machines, and not forgetting useful advice on mending and the after-care of fabrics. Finally, it offers a comprehensive glossary of sewing.

Patterns and templates are included where necessary. The terminology used throughout is UK-standard, together with the corresponding US terms in square brackets [ ] to make this a practical guide for all readers.

It only remains to wish everyone Happy Sewing!

CUTTING TOOLS

Invest in the best quality shears and scissors that you can afford and don't allow anyone – including yourself – to blunt [dull] them by cutting paper, card, string or sticky tape. Look for blades secured with an adjustable screw rather than a rivet and have them professionally sharpened from time to time. Lefthanded scissors and shears are widely available through the internet.

Dressmakers' and tailors' shears have asymmetric handles and long blades for cutting smoothly through fabric at a low angle on a flat surface. Chrome-plated steel shears are the most durable but fairly heavy. There are lighter versions in stainless steel with coloured plastic handles.

Pinking shears make a scalloped or zigzag cut, producing a readymade seam finish that saves binding or oversewing.

Sewing scissors equipped with 15 cm [6 in] blades are the most useful size for your workbox. They have equal thumb and finger holes, and are used for trimming and clipping seams.

Embroidery scissors are used not only by embroiderers but for precision cutting in other needlecrafts such as tapestry and quilting. The blades are 3–10 cm [1¼–4 in] in length and so sharply pointed that it is safest to keep them in a case.

A seam ripper, as its name implies, is the most effective tool for opening seams and removing machine stitching. Use with care because it is all too easy to pierce the surrounding fabric.

THE SEWING MACHINE

Your single most important item of sewing equipment, a well-built sewing machine – whether it's a cast iron heirloom or the latest computerized model – will give you decades of service so long as it is properly used and maintained.

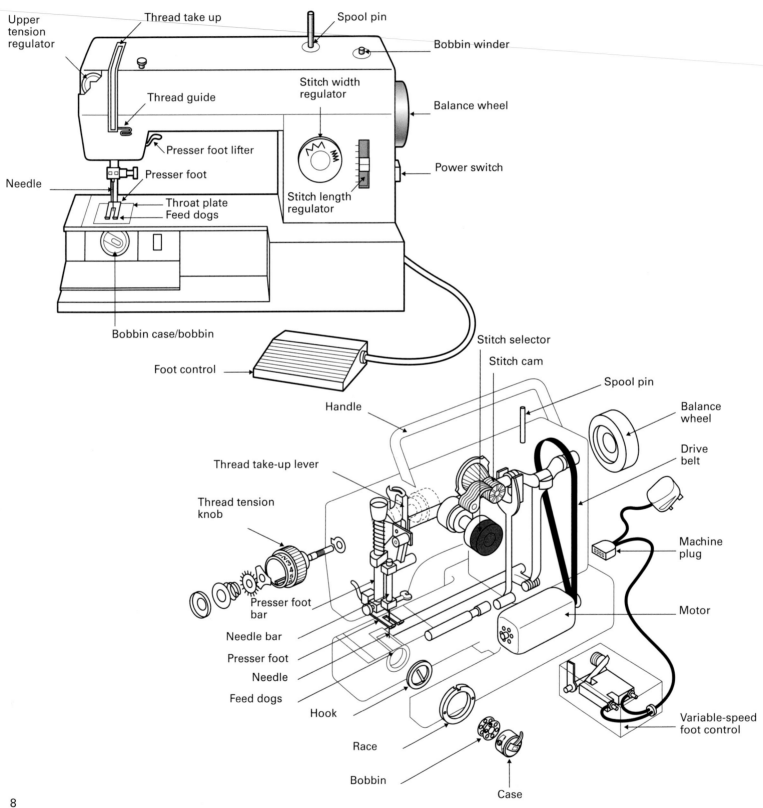

Upper tension regulator
Thread take up
Spool pin
Bobbin winder
Thread guide
Stitch width regulator
Balance wheel
Presser foot lifter
Power switch
Needle
Presser foot
Throat plate
Feed dogs
Stitch length regulator
Bobbin case/bobbin
Foot control
Handle
Stitch selector
Stitch cam
Spool pin
Balance wheel
Drive belt
Thread take-up lever
Thread tension knob
Machine plug
Presser foot bar
Motor
Needle bar
Presser foot
Needle
Feed dogs
Hook
Variable-speed foot control
Race
Bobbin
Case

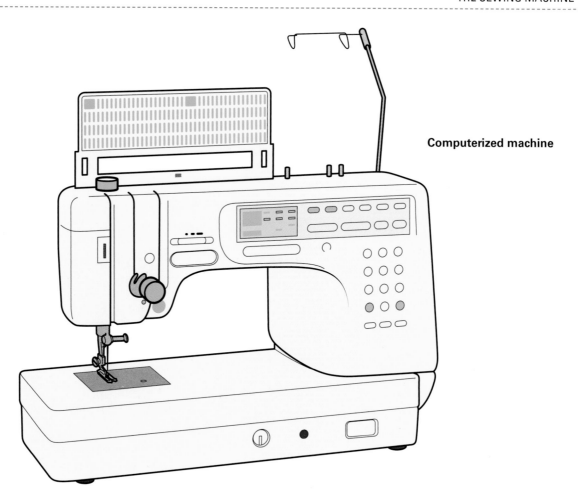

Computerized machine

Buying new or secondhand, your choice will follow the kind of user you are. As a beginner or occasional sewer, look no further than a basic electric model (shown opposite) powered by an electric motor that drives the needle, bobbin and feed dogs, and operated by a foot pedal that controls sewing speed and fabric feed. It will sew different sizes of straight, hem, stretch and zigzag stitches selected at the twist of a dial, as well as button holes and a range of decorative stitches.

Computerized sewing machines are controlled by microchips and several internal motors, making them extremely versatile and a good deal more expensive. Operated using a touchpad and LCD display, with or without a foot or knee pedal, these are sophisticated machines.

The fact that they can memorize and reproduce past tasks and offer hundreds of different stitches via downloads from a PC also indicates that they are well suited to regular and professional users. If you are a dressmaker, run an alteration and repair service, make soft furnishings or do complex embroidery, they are a worthwhile investment.

Prepare a list of the features that you want. Do you need a carrying case or will your machine be kept stationary on a table? Do you prefer a model with hand rather than foot control? Would you like it convertible from a flatbed to free arm access, which makes sewing sleeves easier.

Basic requirements are: a good instruction manual; sturdy construction; bobbin is simple to wind and insert; threading up is straightforward; needles are easily changed; tension and pressure are adjustable; a lever or button for reverse stitching; variable speed control; sews two or more layers of thick fabric without stalling; seam allowance marked on a needle plate; light; thread cutter; minimal oiling, if any.

General purpose machine needles come in sizes 60-120 [8-19]. The finest will stitch delicates and the thickest will cope with tough fabrics like denim. Fit a ballpoint needle for knits or stretch fabrics. Needles inevitably become worn, go blunt [dull] or break. Keep a spare set and change them frequently – ideally after eight hours use or at the start of each major project. The presser foot holds the fabric flat against the feed dogs while the needle makes the stitch. The feed dogs have tiny metal teeth that move the fabric from front to back as the stitching proceeds. The needle plate fits over the feed dogs, covering the bobbin, with a hole for the tip of the needle to pass through.

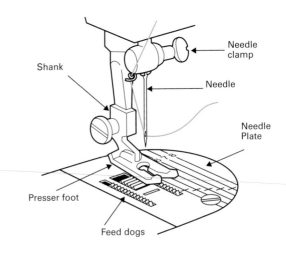

Shank

Needle clamp

Needle

Needle Plate

Presser foot

Feed dogs

MACHINE FEET

The shank of the foot (see 1 below) attaches to the machine with a large screw; newer machines have snap-on feet, which save time. There is an enormous range of interchangeable feet, at least one for every stitch function. Here are five that provide a useful basic kit.

1 Straight-stitch The general purpose presser foot that comes ready to use on most machines.

2 Zigzag Has a horizontal slot to allow for the 'swing' of the needle as it forms a zigzag with the thread.

3 Zipper Used to insert zip fasteners and piping, or anywhere that the stitch line needs to run close. The foot can slide to the left or right, the needle operates in the tiny notch between the foot and the zip.

4 Walking/quilting Uses teeth to feed upper and lower layers of fabric together evenly and avoid

bunching. Ideal for vinyl, velvets, big checks [plaids], and fabrics that tend to slip or stretch.

5 Buttonhole slide The button is placed in the carrier behind the needle and the stitching creates a buttonhole of the right length.

GENERAL CARE AND MAINTENANCE

When not in use, keep a cover on your machine. Regularly clean under the feed dogs and around the bobbin race with a small brush, you will be surprised at the amount of fluff [lint] that gathers there. Oil the machine only according to the maker's instructions and run scrap cotton fabric through afterwards to soak up any excess. Avoid bent or broken needles by raising the needle high before removing work and try not to drag on it while stitching. Sewing with a bent needle will cause it to hit the foot or needle plate and snap. Always raise the presser foot while threading the machine; and lower it when you have finished work completely. As part of the power circuit, treat the foot control with care. Above all, switch power off before disconnecting any plugs or attempting cleaning or repairs.

1

2

3

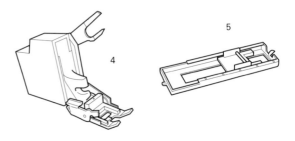

4

5

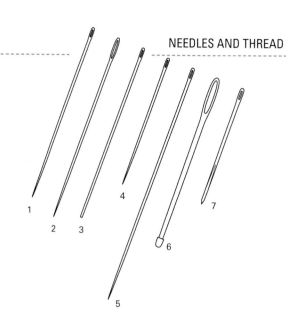

NEEDLES AND THREAD

Hand sewing needles are manufactured in a wide range of lengths and thicknesses; the higher the number the finer the needle. Choose the right needle for the job from the following basic list:

1 Sharps Medium-length and pointed, with a round eye, for general sewing with standard cotton or polyester thread.

2 Crewel or embroidery Pointed like sharps but with a long oval eye like a tapestry needle, for thicker or multiple threads.

3 Blunt-tipped Used for sewing knitted items, designed not to split the yarn.

4 Betweens Very short and sharp, with a small round eye. Used for fine stitching and quilting.

5 Milliner's or straws Very long and thin, with a round eye, for decorative work and trims.

6 Bodkin Large, blunt-tipped, with an eye large enough to carry cord, elastic or ribbon through loops and casings.

7 Glover's or leather Sharp, with a 3-sided tip for piercing leather and PVC without tearing.

Most needles are nickel plated. Gold and platinum plated needles don't discolour or rust but are more expensive. The sand inside an emery cushion will smooth and polish needles and pins when they are pushed into it.

Pins made of hardened steel or brass will not rust, the smallest and finest are ideal for delicate fabrics. Coloured plastic heads make pins easier to see and handle. Keep a large, flat-based pin cushion for general work; a small wrist cushion is better when fitting garments or soft furnishings.

Choose a thread to suit your fabric. Silk (an animal fibre) is best for sewing woollens and silks. Cotton thread matches linen, cotton and rayon (all plant fibres); it has little 'give' and is always best on a tightly woven fabric. By contrast, nylon (polyamide) and polyester threads stretch and recover well, so they are suited to stitching synthetic and knit fabrics; polyester will also stitch wool. Button thread is a useful heavy duty thread.

Sewing threads are spun like knitting yarn by twisting two or more plys together; the tighter the twist, the smoother and stronger the thread will be. It can be natural or man-made, or a combination. Pure cotton has largely been replaced by cotton-covered polyester, where a polyester core provides strength and stretchability while an outer layer of mercerised cotton makes it smoother to work with.

We can still buy specialist threads of pure silk, linen and gold. However, modern manufacturing processes have given us rayon, nylon, polyester, and metal fibre at more modest prices.

Although most modern threads will tolerate machine washing, drying and ironing, bear in mind that some rayons can shrink in a hot wash, while nylon and metallic threads will melt in direct contact with a hot iron.

If you do a lot of hand sewing and want to work more quickly, draw your thread across a block of beeswax (p. 6) to stop it from getting tangled or frayed. The wax will also kill any static electricity from polyester fleece and other synthetics.

FABRIC

Fabrics are manufactured from natural or man-made fibres, often mixed to combine their best qualities. For example, polyester cotton is equally comfortable but creases less than pure cotton; and the warmth of a woollen coat is complemented by the hard-wearing properties of nylon. There are three types of weave on which all woven fabrics are based:

 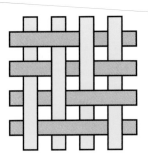 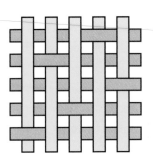

1 Plain weave is the simplest type, where alternate warp (lengthwise) threads go over one and under one of the weft (crosswise) threads. Muslin. calico, taffeta and poplin are all familiar examples.

2 Twill weave interlaces warp and weft threads over and under two or more threads progressively. This produces a clear diagonal pattern on the surface of tough-wearing fabrics like drill, gabardine or denim.

3 Satin weave's smooth surface is created by long warp 'floats' that leave no weft visible. If the floats are formed by the weft threads, it is called 'sateen'. Either way, the glossy surface tends to snag.

THE GRAIN

The grain is the direction in which the warp and weft threads lie. The warp runs lengthwise, parallel to the selvedge. The weft follows the crosswise grain, at right angles to the selvedge. Check the grain before laying out a paper pattern (p. 51). It usually runs lengthwise on garments and curtains.

THE BIAS

The bias lies along any diagonal line between the lengthwise and crosswise grains. True bias is at 45 degrees where you get maximum stretch. Strips cut on the bias are used for facings and bindings around necklines and armholes; they also make piping (p 59).

Shrinkage The tighter the weave, the less likely a fabric is to shrink. However, if it is not pre-shrunk you must put it through the appropriate wash cycle before cutting out. If using a lining or backing fabric, remember to preshrink that too.

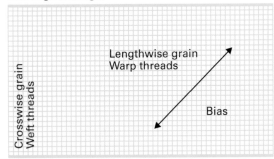

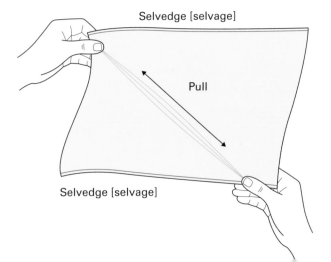

Evenweave

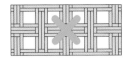
Aida

FABRICS FOR COUNTED THREAD EMBROIDERY

The most widely used fabrics for cross stitch are aida and evenweave. Aida is a block weave favoured by beginners because of its visible stitch holes. Evenweave (frequently linen or cotton) has the same number of threads per inch counted vertically and horizontally, which keeps the cross stitches square and even.

Canvas

You can cross stitch with tapestry wool or stranded cotton [floss] on starched cotton or linen canvas. There are four mesh sizes, compatible with any stitch chart (count the holes in canvas work, not the threads).

Canvas comes as both single thread mesh (mono) and double (duo), also called Penelope canvas.

Plastic canvas

Plastic mesh is usually stitched with 4-ply or double knitting [worsted] wool. Being rigid, it can be pre-cut for making into items such as boxes, place mats, or Christmas decorations.

KNIT FABRIC

Knit fabric is made from interlocking looped stitches, so cut edges don't unravel and the material doesn't crease readily. Knits aren't always stretchy, but those containing spandex (Lycra) fibres stretch length- and crosswise, making them perfect for dance and sportswear. There are two main types of knit: weft and warp knitting (also called 'raschel').

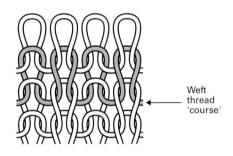
Weft thread 'course'

Warp thread 'wale'

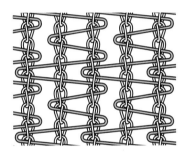

Raschel This type of warp knit has an open construction that imitates lace and hand crochet, with heavy, textured inlaid threads held in place by a much finer yarn.

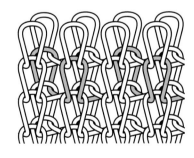

Interlock A smooth warp knit with closely interlocking stitches that allow it to stretch; it's typically used in the manufacture of underwear and casual clothes.

1 Weft knit fabric is produced like hand knitting by working a single yarn in 'courses' or rows across the width of the fabric. Made on a variety of industrial or domestic knitting machines, the 'course' construction means it can be unravelled from one loose end.

2 Warp knit fabric is formed by multiple strands of yarn making loops vertically in individual 'wales' or columns. A specialized machine produces a firm fabric that doesn't ladder. Warp-knitted products include tee shirts, lace curtaining and blankets.

HAND SEWING STITCHES

There are not very many stitches in the plain hand sewing repertoire but each one of them is useful in different situations and worth learning to do well. It is best not to work with your thread too long because it will get tangled. About 35 cm [14 in] is long enough, although tacking [basting] thread may be more.

TACKING [BASTING]

Tacking serves to hold fabric in position until the final stitching is done. It's similar to running stitch but longer. Start with a knot, which you will cut off when the time comes to remove your tacking. There is a soft cotton thread made specially for the job but most people just use ordinary thread in a bright contrasting colour, so they can pick it out afterwards.

RUNNING STITCH

This is the simplest and most basic of stitches, used for seams and gathers (p. 46) and attaching appliqué shapes. First secure the thread with two small stitches on the spot. With the needle at the front, push into the fabric and out again in one move and pull the thread through. Both stitch and space should be of equal length. Fasten off with a back stitch.

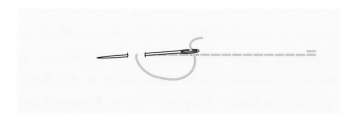

BACK STITCH

This imitates machine sewing and is just as strong. Begin exactly as for running stitch then sew back over the first space. Needle out again at one stitch space ahead of the last one that you made. Repeat the process, pushing the needle back in again at the point where the previous stitch ended.

HOLBEIN OR DOUBLE RUNNING STITCH

When completed, this looks like backstitch but is actually constructed from two passes of running stitch, where the second pass returns and precisely fills the gaps left by the first. This makes the back appear much neater than that of backstitch and it's ideal for double-sided items such as hand-sewn bookmarks and Christmas tree decorations.

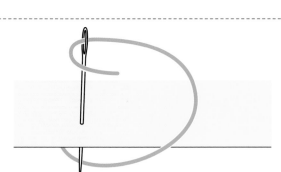

BLANKET STITCH

1 Secure thread on the wrong side (WS) and bring through at the edge of the fabric. Needle in at the desired stitch height and width to the right. Needle out again directly below.

2 Pass the needle forwards through the loop, forming a half-hitch, and tighten the thread against the fabric edge. Repeat to form a row. Fasten off with an extra half-hitch around the final loop.

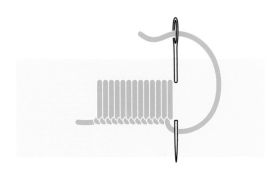

BUTTONHOLE STITCH

With the same basic construction as blanket stitch, this stitch evolved to seal the raw edges of a buttonhole. Stitched closely like satin stitch (p. 66), it can be used to neaten both straight and curved edges and features in cutwork embroidery such as broderie anglaise.

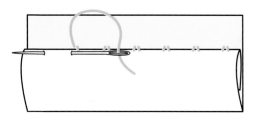

SLIP STITCH

Used for stitching a folded edge invisibly to a flat surface. Catch up a few threads of flat fabric with your needle, enter the fold and slide along inside for up to 1 cm [½ in] before emerging to make the next stitch.

LADDER STITCH

This stitch joins fabric edges together in a concealed flat seam. If possible, first iron down the opening with the seam allowances folded under. This will give two distinct folds to stitch into from side to side. If you are closing the gap on a stuffed toy, use a strong thread or double your ordinary sewing cotton to take the extra pressure. Keep your stitches fairly close together.

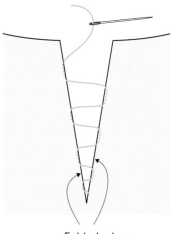

Folded edges

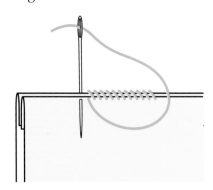

WHIP STITCH OR OVERSEWING

A fast, easy stitch used for sewing items together at the edges. First, secure the thread with two small stitches on the spot and continue with neat diagonal stitches equally spaced. This stitch can be done from left to right or vice versa.

FELT GLOVE PUPPET
LEVEL BEGINNER

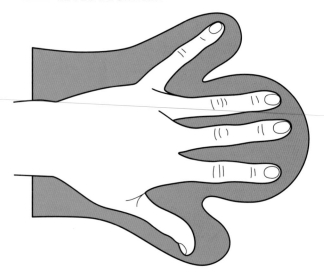

1 Pin two felt squares together and draw round your hand with a fabric marker. Allow plenty of room for movement. This is the basic glove shape.

2 Cut out both layers together and join them with neat blanket stitch (p 15). Remember to leave an opening for your hand!

3 Copy or trace Tiger's features and cut them from different coloured felts (see template p.118). Use the photograph as a guide to the black stripes.

4 First arrange the features without glue. Then fix them with the PVA in the following order:

5 Glue brown inner ears to white outer ears and attach to either side of the head with three short black stripes stuck between.

6 Glue black inner eye to green outer eye and attach eyes below ears.

7 Position four remaining head stripes to frame the face, use the photograph as a guide.

8 Glue white cheeks on top of white chin to form muzzle, leaving a narrow gap for the centre nose. Attach muzzle to lower face.

9 Stick brown nose on top of muzzle.

10 Stick two large pink pads in the centre of either paw. Surround each pad with four pink toes.

11 Two short black stripes mark the base of Tiger's 'arms'. Finally add the longest stripes to the rest of his body.

Human characters are easily created by sewing face and hands to the basic glove. Glue on or embroider the features.

YOU WILL NEED

- Two 30 cm [12 in] felt squares in your chosen base colour
- Smaller pieces of black, white, brown, green and pink for Tiger features
- Optional 15 cm [6 in] felt square in skin colour for a 'human' character
- Matching threads
- PVA fabric glue
- Small pointed scissors for details

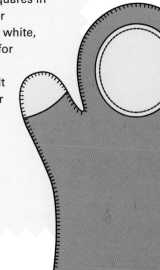

SEWING AN OPEN SEAM

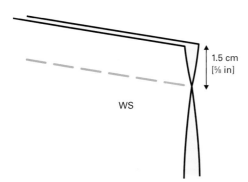

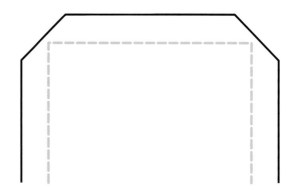

1 Pin and tack [baste] right sides together before stitching a line of running or back stitch 15 mm [⅝ in] from the edge of the fabric, this margin is called the seam allowance.

TRIMMING CORNERS

For example at the bottom of a bag or the ends of a waistband, cut away excess fabric as close to the stitching as possible in order to turn out a sharp, right-angled corner. Use a crochet hook or knitting needle to help you but nothing sharp that will damage the fabric.

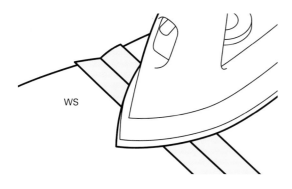

2 Lay joined pieces out flat and press the seam allowance open with an iron.

TOPSTITCHING

Topstitching is frequently used to reinforce seam lines where extra strength is required, such as on bag handles. It can also be used for purely decorative purposes, for example in a contrasting colour around lapels and pockets. Use a longer machine stitch than for ordinary seam sewing.

Use a straight-stitch or an open toe (p. 27) machine foot. Ordinary all-purpose thread can be used for topstitching on most fabrics. However, if you are using a very lightweight fabric or something as heavy as a blanket, choose finer or thicker thread accordingly. Thread weights are numbered – just like needles – the higher the number the finer the thread.

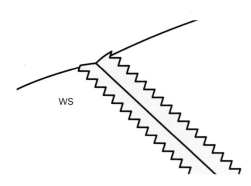

3 Use pinking shears if necessary to neaten raw edges and prevent fraying. Alternatively, edges may be blanket-stitched or oversewn (p. 15).

If you have no thick thread, it is possible to use two ordinary top threads together instead. Simply put a reel on each spool pin and thread up the machine as normal. If you have only one spool pin, then fill two bobbins and place one on top of the other with a circle of felt between them so they revolve at the same speed.

SIMPLE TOTE BAG

LEVEL BEGINNER

This is a child-size tote, 22.8 x 20.3 cm [9 x 8 in], but the basic proportions and method can be used to make totes of any size. Lining is optional, although it will add extra strength, and pockets can also be added, inside or out.

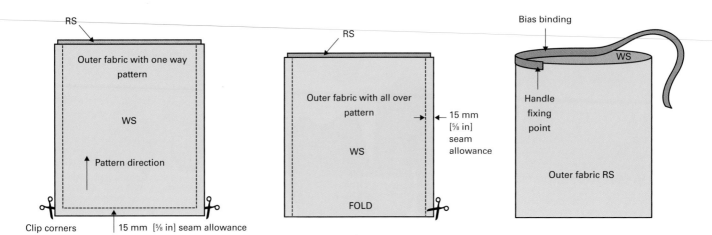

1 For outer fabric with a one-way pattern, cut in half and place right sides (RS) together. Check pattern is upright on both pieces. Pin, tack [baste] and sew around sides and base with a 15 mm [⅝ in] seam allowance. For outer fabric that is plain or has an all-over pattern, fold in half with RS together. Tack and sew up the sides with a 15 mm [⅝ in] seam allowance. Clip corners, turn RS out and iron.

2 Start at a point to be covered by a handle (about 5 cm [2 in] from the side seam), fold the bias binding in half and tack around the top of the outer bag, enclosing the raw edge. Overlap ends by 12 mm [½ in].

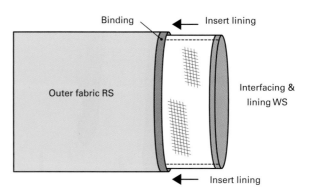

YOU WILL NEED

- Outer fabric with one-way pattern 56.5 x 23.5 cm [22¼ x 9¼ in]
- OR Outer fabric with all-over pattern or plain 53.3 x 23.5 cm [21 x 9¼ in]
- Lining fabric with all-over pattern or plain 45.5 x 23.5 cm [18 x 9¼ in]
- Interfacing (eg Vilene) 45.5 x 23.5 cm [18 x 9¼ in]
- 50 cm [19 in] bias binding 2.5 cm [1 in] wide
- 81.5 cm [32 in] herringbone tape 2.5 cm [1 in] wide for handles
- Matching thread

3 Attach interfacing to wrong side (WS) of lining fabric. Stitch down long sides only with 5 mm [³⁄₁₆ in] seam allowance, leaving short sides open. If you want, this is the time to top-stitch a pocket to the lining.

4 RS together, fold lining in half and sew up the sides with 15 mm [⅝ in] seam allowance. Trim allowance down to 1 cm [⅜ in] but do not turn RS out. Slide lining into outer bag and push down until lower corners meet. The lining will be about 3.8 cm [1½ in] shorter than the outer bag.

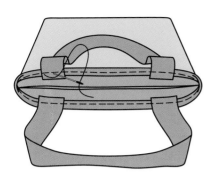

5 Cut herringbone tape in half and, measuring 3.5 cm [1⅜ in] in from the side seams, tack 12 mm [½ in] of each handle end to WS top edge of outer bag.

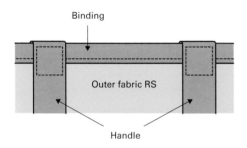

6 Machine stitch around the binding, including the handles in one go. Flip handles back to RS of outer bag and secure with reinforcing squares of machine stitching.

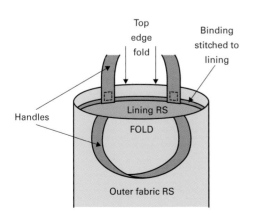

7 Fold the top 3.8 cm [1½ in] inwards over the raw edges of lining and interfacing. Slip hem the binding closely to the lining fabric for a neat, firm finish.

BUTTONED CUSHION COVER
LEVEL BEGINNER/INTERMEDIATE

A removable cover in two different fabrics, to fit a 40.5 cm [16 in] square cushion. For a larger cushion increase fabric length and breadth accordingly. Altering one dimension only will produce a rectangular cover.

1 With right sides (RS) facing, tack [baste] the fabrics together along one short edge. Machine stitch with a seam allowance of 1.5 cm [⅝ in].

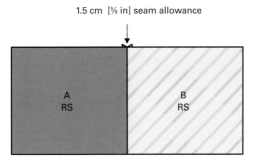

1.5 cm [⅝ in] seam allowance

2 On the wrong side (WS), press the seam to one side, away from A. Fabric A will carry the false fastening. Fabric B will overlap A with three working buttonholes.

3 Turn back to the RS and create a false opening by folding fabric A 2.5 cm [1 in] over the seam line and back on itself. Press lightly, using a cloth to prevent the seam showing through.

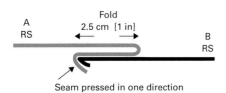

Fold
2.5 cm [1 in]
A RS
B RS
Seam pressed in one direction

4 To hold the fold at either end, machine two short lines of stitching, 5 mm [³⁄₁₆ in] in from the sides.

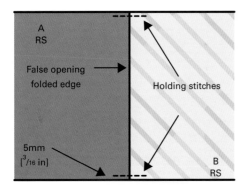

A RS
False opening folded edge
Holding stitches
5mm [³⁄₁₆ in]
B RS

5 RS of fabric B, measure 39.5 cm [15⅝ in] from A's folded edge and iron a turning at the free end. WS, fold the raw edge under once more and stitch down each side to hold. This forms the overlap that carries the buttonholes.

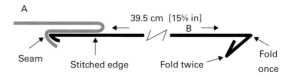

A
39.5 cm [15⅝ in]
B
Seam   Stitched edge   Fold twice   Fold once

6 Mark positions of three buttonholes, using tacking thread.

7 On RS of fabric A, measure 46 cm [18 in] from the edge of the false opening and iron a single turning at the free end. Place iron-on interfacing inside the turning, with adhesive side against the raw edge, and iron again. The interfacing prevents fraying and supports the three working buttons.

8 Lay cover flat, RS up. Measure 19.5 cm [7¾ in] each way from the edge of the false opening and fold up both ends so they overlap 4 cm [1½ in] on WS. Check that the joins line up with each another so the cover appears symmetrical from the side when filled (see opposite above).

YOU WILL NEED

- Two contrasting pieces of fabric, A and B, each 53.5 x 46 cm [21 x 18 in]
- A strip of iron-on interfacing 4 x 46 cm [1½ x 18 in]
- Six buttons 2.5 cm [1 in] diameter
- Matching threads
- Pinking shears OR 1 metre [yard] of 2.5 cm [1 in] bias binding for main side seams
- Embroidery scissors for the buttonholes
- Fabric marker pen

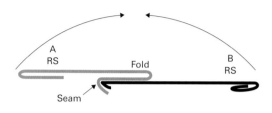

9 Pin, tack and stitch both sides of the folded cover with a 2.5 cm [1 in] seam allowance. Clip corners. Use pinking shears to trim allowance down to 1.5 cm [⅝ in], levelling all folds and overlaps. If fraying badly, enclose the seams with binding instead (p. 40).

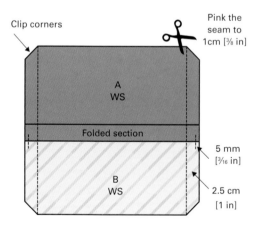

10 Turn the cover RS out. By hand (or machine, see p. 71), cut and sew three buttonholes 1 cm [⅜ in] from the opening edge of fabric B.

11 To make an accurate cut in the fabric, add the button width to its thickness, plus 3 mm [⅛ in] for ease. Set a pin at each end and tack [baste] or draw a line between the two. Using very sharp embroidery scissors or a seam ripper, pierce the fabric mid-line and cut outwards.

12 Overcast cut edges to prevent fraying. Make four stitches down each side of the buttonhole, about 3 mm [⅛ in] deep.

13 Hold the buttonhole as flat as you can while sewing. Buttonhole stitch is similar to blanket (p. 15) but stitched more closely. Work to the same depth for neatness.

14 Mark the position of the buttonholes and attach working buttons to the opening on fabric A.

15 Sew three buttons onto the false opening. Match the spacing to that of the working buttons.

SEWING AN ENCASED SEAM

Encased seams, such as the French seam, enclose allowances so that no raw edges are left visible. They are suitable for unlined garments, lingerie and sheer fabrics that tend to fray. The double stitching stands up well to frequent wear and washing.

SEWING A FRENCH SEAM BY HAND

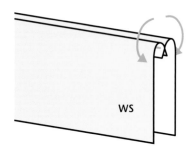

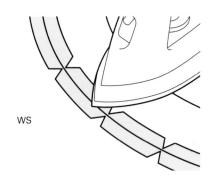

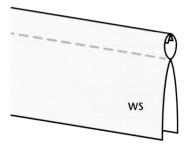

1 Pin and tack [baste] wrong sides together before stitching a line of running or back stitch 10 mm [⅜ in] from the edge of the fabric.

2 Trim both layers of seam allowance to 3 mm [⅛ in] and fold right sides of the fabric together down the stitched line. Press along the fold, enclosing the trimmed seam allowance.

3 Stitch a second line 6 mm [¼ in] from fold and press the finished seam to one side

CURVES AND CORNERS
CLIPPING OUTER AND INNER CURVES

Curved seams naturally give rise to curved seam allowances, which have to be clipped to allow them to stretch or fold together neatly and lie flat.

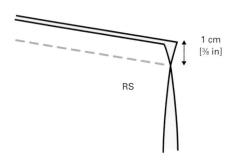

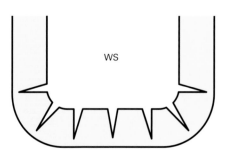

Necklines, armholes [armscyes] and pockets are all places where curves are clipped. If you have to clip down to the stitch line, be careful not to cut the stitching itself. If necessary afterwards, use the tip of the iron to press the seam around the curve.

Single cuts at regular intervals may be enough to ease together silk or cotton lawn, but to avoid bulking up on thicker fabrics, cut wedge-shaped notches into the seam allowance and remove the excess completely.

HEMMING
TURNING A HEM

Hemming is frequently done by hand, even when the rest of a garment is machine stitched.

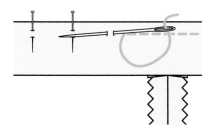

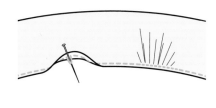

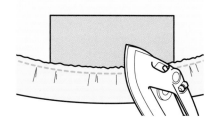

1 Pin up the hem, then tack [baste] the lower edge and turn the raw edge over at the top, ready to stitch. If the fabric is fraying or too thick, sew tape around the right side of the raw edge and hem stitch onto that (p. 40).

2 For a flared or circular hem, ease fullness with running stitch around the top edge. Pull up regular groups of gathers using a pin, then tack [baste] in preparation for stitching. Alternatively, attach bias tape (p. 40) after gathering.

3 Steam pressing heavy woollen fabric before stitching helps to reduce hem fullness. Use a cloth to avoid making a ridge on the front of the fabric. Press very lightly and lift the iron clear, do not drag it across damp fabric.

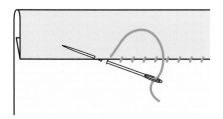

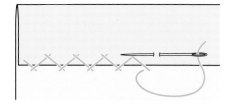

Hemming stitch
The second turn of the hem should be narrower than the first, about 7-10 mm [¼ - ⅜ in]. Secure thread with two small stitches on the edge of this fold. Begin hemming by picking up two or three threads of the main fabric before passing the needle up to catch the fold again. This stitch can be worked from right or left.

Herringbone (Catchstitch) flat hem
Secures hems on thick, non-fraying fabrics where no second turning is made. It is basically a large cross stitch formed by making a back stitch alternately in each layer of fabric.

Rolled hem
For delicate fabrics: first stitch along a marked hemline with a fine needle. Trim to within 5 mm [³⁄₁₆ in] of that line and, between thumb and forefinger, start rolling the raw edge over the stitching. Insert your needle through the roll, catch a thread or two in the main fabric and slide the needle into the roll again. Every few stitches draw up thread to secure roll.

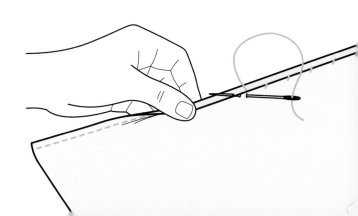

CASINGS

A casing is a tube for elastic, cord or ribbon. Stretch waistbands and drawstring bags use casings. In home furnishing, a casing may take a curtain rod or wire.

MAKING A CASING

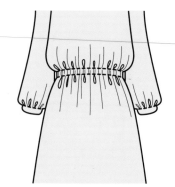

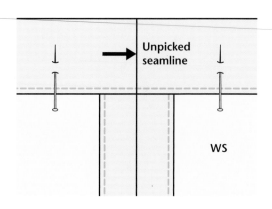

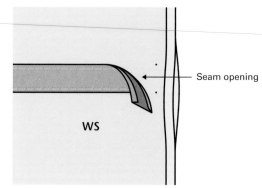

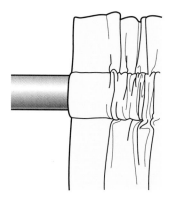

1 Fold fabric over twice, like a hem. Pin, then stitch. If hand sewing, use back stitch for strength. To leave a gap for drawstrings, unpick both side seams above the horizontal stitch line, leave the seam allowance turned inside.

2 Alternatively, create a channel with straight tape. Sewn onto the wrong side of the fabric, it should be a little wider than the elastic, ribbon or cord going through it. Make use of any seam openings to thread the elastic etc. but close them separately without blocking the channel.

THREADING THE CASING

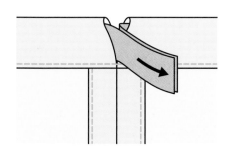

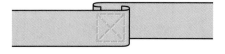

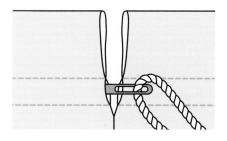

1 Calculate how much elastic you need by stretching it around the waist, wrist etc., allow extra for sewing the ends. Safety-pin the free end to the fabric before threading; the casing will gather up as you go. Level the ends outside the casing when threading is done, pin together and check for fit.

2 Trim any excess if necessary, then join the elastic as shown. Stitch a square and/or a cross for a really firm hold. The waistband, cuff etc. can then be closed.

3 A two-way drawstring, buy enough cord to go twice round the top of the bag, plus about 30 cm [12 in]. The casing should have a gap in the seam on each side. Cut the cord in half and thread each half right around the casing, starting and finishing on opposite sides. Knot the cord ends together tightly. Pull both sides at once to close the bag.

ORGANZA FAVOUR BAG
LEVEL BEGINNER

This little bag measures 10 x 15 cm [4 x 6 in] and can be hand or machine sewn to hold favours for parties, weddings or naming ceremonies. Made from muslin or lawn, it could also hold a sachet of lavender or cedar wood to scent a cupboard or drawer.

YOU WILL NEED

• Piece of organza 13 x 40.5 cm [5¼ x 16 in]
• 25 cm [10 in] silk, satin or nylon ribbon 15 mm [⅝ in] wide for casing
• 65 cm [26 in] matching ribbon 7 mm [¼ in] wide for two-way drawstring
• Or same quantity of thin silky cord

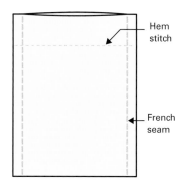

Hem stitch

French seam

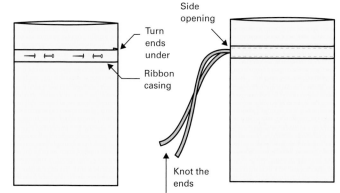

Turn ends under

Ribbon casing

Side opening

Knot the ends

1 Fold over 5 cm [2 in] on each end of the fabric and machine stitch or slip hem turnings as shown on p 23. Fold hemmed fabric in half with wrong sides facing.

2 Make an encased seam on each side of the bag (see p 22). When seams are done, turn bag right side out, ready to apply casing to the outside.

3 Cut casing ribbon in half. Take one piece, turn raw ends under and pin across one side of the bag, concealing the line of hem stitches. Either machine stitch or create a channel with small, even running stitches (p 14) along each edge of the ribbon. Repeat and match with remaining ribbon on the other side.

4 You have left a narrow opening in the casing on either side of the bag. Cut your drawstring ribbon or cord in half and use a bodkin or small safety pin to thread it right around the casing (see method opposite). Knot the ends together. Repeat from opposite side with remaining ribbon or cord.

Place the favours inside and draw up ribbons or cord to close. Before you fill the bag, you might like to decorate it with embroidery, lace or beads.

INTRODUCING APPLIQUÉ

Appliqué is the technique of cutting a shape from one fabric and stitching it to another, either by hand or machine.

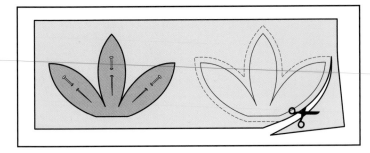

1 Pin template to fabric and trace round with a fabric marker. Cut shape out with 7 mm [¼ in] seam allowance; no allowance is necessary if planning to oversew (3).

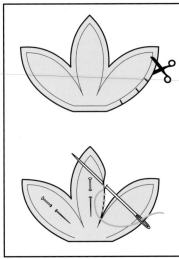

2 Clip curves for a smooth edge when slip-stitching (p. 15) appliqué to base fabric. Turn seam allowance under with your needle tip as you sew.

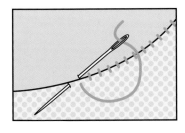

3 You can oversew raw edges directly on to the base fabric. Stitch closely if the shape frays.

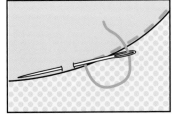

4 Running stitch can be used for attaching non-fraying material such as felt.

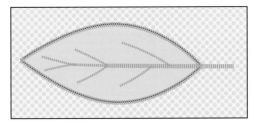

5 Appliqué by machine offers zigzag, buttonhole and satin stitch.

SCALING IMAGES

Found images are rarely the exact size we want. This is a method of scaling shapes up and down in size. Reverse size order in Steps 1 and 2 to enlarge the image.

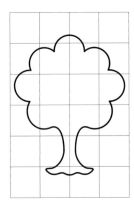

1 Trace or print out the original image. Enclose outline in a frame and divide the area into squares.

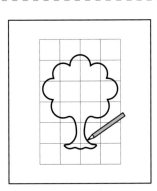

2 Rule up a smaller sheet into same number of divisions and copy the original, square by square, until the reduced design is complete and ready to form a template.

USING FUSIBLE WEB

Fusible web is a fine mesh impregnated with heat-sensitive glue that sticks one piece of fabric to another when ironed. It has a paper backing that you can draw on.

It also prevents the appliqué fraying and with the motif trimmed to shape, it keeps cut edges looking sharp without the need to turn them under. Some brands carry a lot of glue, which can make the fabric difficult to stitch, so pick one with a medium-strength bond.

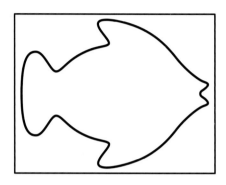

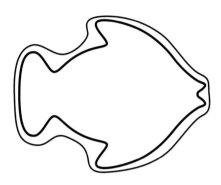

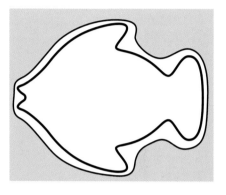

1 Draw or trace a motif onto the paper side of the fusible web. If it is asymmetrical, like this fish, make it a mirror image (reverse left to right).

2 With a margin of about 7 mm [¼ in], roughly cut the shape out of the web.

3 Place cut-out on WS of appliqué fabric, paper side uppermost, and iron to fuse surfaces together. When cool, cut out carefully along the drawn lines

Peel off the paper backing. There may be backing on both sides, brands vary; always read the manufacturer's instructions. Position the prepared appliqué, RS up, onto your background fabric and press again. It's wise to use a pressing cloth to keep any glue off your iron.

Fusible web creates only a temporary bond, tending to lift and curl after washing. So it is still necessary to hand- or machine-sew the appliquéd shape into place using a satin stitch, blanket stitch or several lines of straight stitching.

MACHINE ACCESSORIES

Open toe appliqué A useful variation on the standard zigzag foot, the widely spaced toes afford a clear view of the work in progress.

Appliqué/embroidery A useful variation on the standard zigzag foot, the toes on this foot are shorter, for smoother stitching, improved visibility and manoeuvrability. It is particularly suited to appliqué.

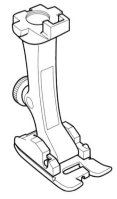

USING FREEZER PAPER

Freezer paper, first invented as food wrapping, is now generally available from quilting suppliers. Lightly waxed on one side, on the other side it's untreated and looks and feels like ordinary paper. You can draw on the matt (non-shiny) side, cut out your shape and it will adhere to fabric when ironed shiny side down. It doesn't harm the iron and is the modern equivalent of using traditional paper templates.

Freezer paper templates allow for greater accuracy and make handling of shapes much easier. Quilters' freezer paper is also the right size for photocopiers and printers, so you can create multiples of any one shape. If using printer ink, check first whether it is washable, in case it marks your fabric.

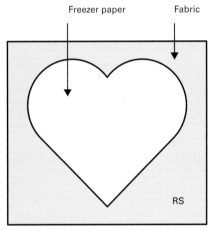

Freezer paper   Fabric

RS

1 A heart shape is ideal for practice: trace, draw, photocopy or print onto the matt side of the freezer paper then, using an ironing board, lay the paper shiny side down on the RS of your fabric. Press with a hot dry iron. The paper will adhere to the fabric in a few seconds. Cut out the heart shape with a margin of 7 mm [¼ in] and peel the paper off.

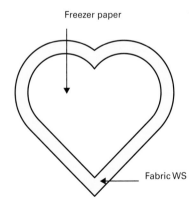

Freezer paper

Fabric WS

2 Place the fabric heart WS up on the board and reposition the paper, shiny side up.

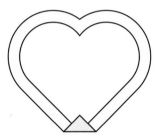

3 Press the point of the heart up with the tip or edge of the iron. Make sure it sticks to the paper.

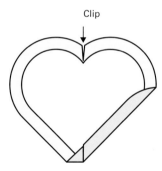

Clip

4 Clip curves where necessary. Continue to press the fold-over margin on to the paper all around the heart.

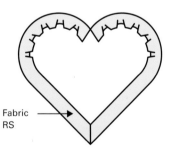

Fabric RS

5 If the paper lifts away, re-apply the iron and then hold firmly with your fingertips until the paper cools.

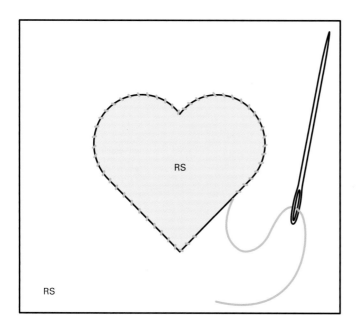

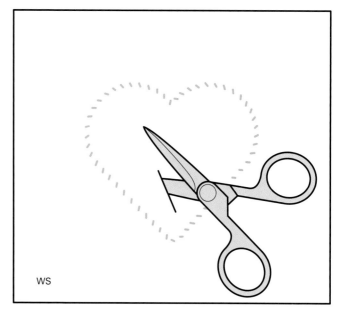

6 Pin the heart to the backing fabric, RS up. Sew with a 'stabbing' motion, bringing the needle straight up vertically through the appliquéd shape and going back down through the backing. The stitches should be quite close together. Avoid piercing the freezer paper if possible, so that it can be more easily removed later. If you leave a gap of about 2.5 cm [1 in] you may be able to remove the paper from a small shape by working it out through the gap with a pair of tweezers. Finally, sew the gap close.

Sewing by machine Use an appliqué foot (p. 27) if available, as it enables you to see more clearly where the stitches are. Set to a very small zigzag stitch, or use the machine hemstitch, which employs a sequence of several straight stitches, then a zigzag. With the hemstitch, the straight stitches should go into the background fabric only, as close as possible to the edge of the appliqué.

7 On the WS and cut a slit in the backing fabric and gently pull the freezer paper out through the slit. Be careful not to pierce the heart shape with the tip of the scissors. There is usually no real need to sew up this slit since the piece will either be lined or become the top layer of a quilt sandwich where the reverse will not be seen. When done, press very lightly.

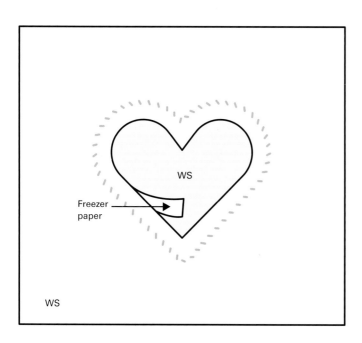

8 For larger areas, it is best to cut away all the backing fabric that lies immediately behind the appliqué, leaving a 7 mm [¼ in] seam allowance. Again, take care not to pierce the actual heart shape with the scissors. Gently pull out the freezer paper, not forgetting to strip out the pieces under the seam. Finally, press very lightly.

APPLIQUÉD SHOE BAG
LEVEL INTERMEDIATE

The basic drawstring bag can be made to any size. You'll find the appliqué for this shoe bag on p. 118. Fitting an optional side zip makes it easier to use when hung on a peg.

1 Draw up the shapes to the required size and cut templates from paper. Pin paper shapes to felt and cut them out.

2 Fold fabric in half to 30 x 45 cm [12 x 18 in]. Mark or tack [baste] the halfway line as a guide to placing appliqué.

3 Cut six white felt circles of 8 mm [5/16 in], for eyelets. Cut 12 cm [4¾ in] from each end of the shoelace and a further 2.5 cm [1 in] and 2 cm [¾ in] from the rest. Dab fray stop on ends if necessary.

4 Attach laces to purple felt and fix white circles over the cut ends with a single cross stitch.

5 Assemble the upper as follows: purple base with white heel tip under; white toe cap; green mid-section. Hand-stitch heel tip, toe cap and mid-section to the purple base with small, neat running stitch in appropriate colours. Finally, hand-stitch purple base to bag fabric, or attach by machine with zigzag or buttonhole setting.

6 Centre mauve sole on white and set machine to largest zig-zag stitch. Make two groups of horizontal lines for the sole pattern. Top stitch a purple triangle trademark in the middle.

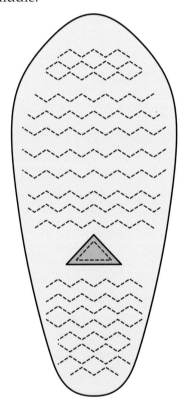

7 Neaten back threads by cutting interfacing to the sole shape and ironing over the back.

8 Using white thread, hand-sew sole to bag fabric using small running stitches around the edge, or attach by machine with zigzag or buttonhole setting.

YOU WILL NEED

- 60 x 45 cm [24 x 18 in] close-woven fabric such as calico or twill
- 20cm [8 in] zip fastener in matching or contrast colour
- 25 cm [10 in] squares of white, mauve, purple and green felt
- One white shoe lace
- 21 x 10 cm [8¼ x 4 in] iron-on interfacing (Vilene)
- One metre [yard] tape or cord for drawstring
- Matching threads
- Embroidery scissors
- Fabric marker

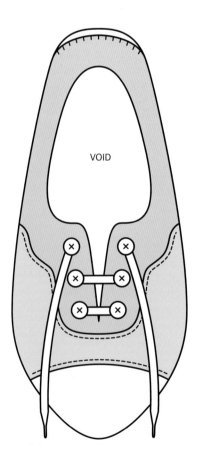

VOID

9 Right sides (RS) together, machine stitch side of bag with 1.5 cm [⅝ in] seam allowance. If fitting a zip fastener, stitch up 5 cm [2 in] from the base, then leave a gap of 20 cm [8 in] and resume stitching to the top. Press seam open, including gap for zip.

10 Fit zip fastener (p. 71). Remove tacking [basting].

11 RS together, machine stitch base with 1.5 cm [⅝ in] seam allowance. For extra strength, run a second line of stitching. Clip the corners.

12 Open top 4 cm [1½ in] of side seam and iron 7mm [¼ in] of the raw edge down on the wrong side (WS). Fold over the remaining 32 mm [1¼ in] tack and stitch to form a casing (p. 24). Leave a slot open at seam for the drawstring. Top-stitch around the fold to make casing 2 cm [¾ in] wide. Remove tacking.

13 Turn bag RS out. With bodkin or safety pin, thread tape or cord through casing and stitch or knot the ends together.

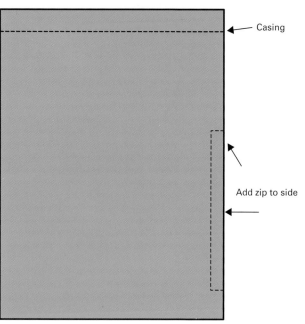

Casing

Add zip to side

BAG KEEPER
LEVEL BEGINNER

Keep plastic carriers tidy and ready to re-use.

YOU WILL NEED

- Fabric for the basic label, cut to the desired size or shape. With thick felt you won't need backing, for anything lighter, cut iron-on interfacing (Vilene) to fit
- Felt for the elephant figure and his bag
- Cotton fabric for the bag keeper itself, 51 x 41 cm [20 x 16 in]
- Elastic 7 mm [¼ in] wide, cut into two lengths, 28 cm [11 in] and 20 cm [8 in]
- Tape or ribbon for the handle, 37.5 cm [15 in] long, 20 mm [¾ in] wide
- PVA fabric glue

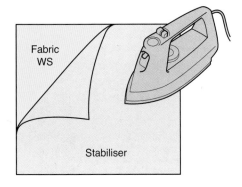

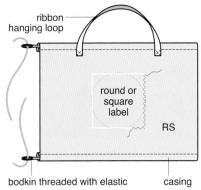

1 Iron Vilene to the wrong side (WS) of the label fabric. The elephant and his bag can be squared up or copied to the size you want and two separate paper templates made (p. 119). Place the templates on the felt and trace around with a fabric marker. Embroidering the words is optional (pp. 66-67).

2 Make a 13 mm [½ in] casing on both long sides of the bag fabric by first folding over 20 mm [¾ in] and then turning the raw edge under again by 7 mm [¼ in]. Tack [baste] turnings and machine stitch close to the folds to form the casings.

3 Cut out and glue elephant and bag to the label. Tack [baste] the label to the centre of the main fabric. Attach with a decorative machine stitch. Fold the raw ends under and sew the handle firmly to the top edge – either inside or out – 17.5 cm [7 in] from each end and below the casing.

4 Run the 28 cm [11 in] elastic through the top casing, gathering fabric as you go. Sew down the ends close to each edge. Repeat for the lower casing, using the 20 cm [8 in] elastic. The lower opening is smaller than the top.

5 Fold the bag fabric in half lengthways, WS out. With a 13 mm [½ in] seam allowance, machine stitch the side, ensuring that the ends of the elastic are securely included. Oversew the seam edges together or enclose with binding tape.

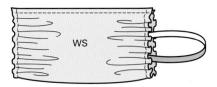

6 Turn the bag RS out and hang up ready for use.

SUNGLASSES CASE
LEVEL ALL LEVELS

Counted thread embroidery worked on block weave fabric. The basic case pattern can be reduced in size to hold a mobile phone or travel card, or adapted for a coin purse or pencil case. The embroidery can be simple or complex, as you wish.

1 Mark the folds on the aida with coloured thread and tack [baste] the halfway guidelines in another colour (see p. 119).

2 Use three or four strands of embroidery cotton [floss] on an 11-count aida, two or three for a 14-count, and two for a 16-count. Cut a length, grip one strand firmly and draw your other hand down taking the remaining threads with you. Lay selected strands straight and smooth them together again. Embroidery twist (also called perle [pearl] thread) is non-divisible, use it as it comes.

YOU WILL NEED

- A strip of 14-count (14 holes per inch) aida (p. 13) 44 x 12 cm [17⅜ x 4¾ in]
- Cotton lining fabric 44 x 12 cm [17⅜ x 4¾ in]
- Non-woven interfacing 44 x 12 cm [17⅜ x 4¾ in]
- 75 cm [29½ in] of 15mm [⅝ in] wide satin bias binding
- Matching threads
- Stranded embroidery cotton [floss] or twist (we used four colours, including one variegated and one metallic, to represent sun, sea and sand)
- Two 7mm [¼ in] snap fasteners (alternatively, Velcro or a button and loop, see p. 58)

3 Lumpy knots at the back spoil your work. Start instead by pushing through from the wrong side (WS) leaving a 3 cm [1¼ in] tail of thread behind. Hold the tail against the cloth and catch it down with new stitches. Fasten off by running thread under three or four WS stitches.

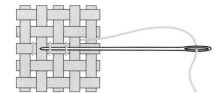

4 Using a blunt-tipped tapestry needle, work outwards from the centre of the design, counting squares as you go. We used a simple arrangement of straight stitches worked end to end in one colour at a time, but cross stitch designs work well too. Allow a 2 cm [¾ in] margin for turnings at either end of the strip.

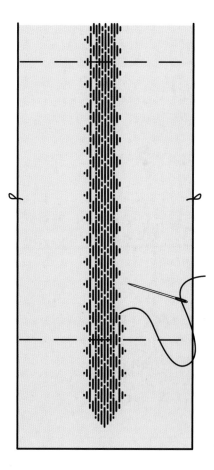

5 The pattern grows.

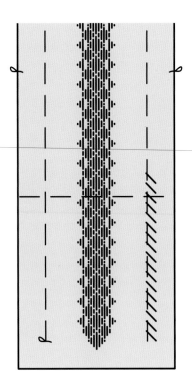

6 Centre strip finished, mark out border with more tacking.

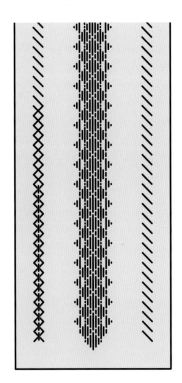

7 Border in progress.

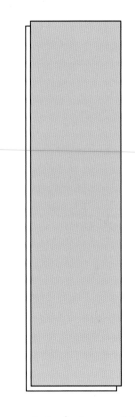

8 Prepare interfacing and lining. Tack interfacing to WS of aida, stitch lengthways only, avoiding embroidered areas.

9 WS together, tack cotton lining to aida, lengthways only, with interfacing between the two.

10 RS out, fold assembled strip once to form bag section.

11 Without pinning or tacking, which could cause puckering, machine steadily down each side of the bag section, with 5 mm [³⁄₁₆ in] seam allowance. Begin each time at the folded end and finish 3-4 cm [1½ in] short of the bag opening. Remove from the machine with 10 cm [4 in] thread ends.

12 Fold the unembroidered margin of aida and the lining inwards towards each other at the opening. Slip stitch the lining a fraction below the folded edge of the aida.

13 Using thread ends, hand stitch the distance to the opening on both sides and loosely sew at points where upper half meets lower, to create relaxed hinges.

14 Restart the line of machine stitching just beyond the opening and carry on to finish 2 cm [¾ in] short of the end of the flap section. Repeat step 12. Remove tacking.

15 Sew two halves of snap fasteners (p. 58) to the flap section without piercing embroidered surface.

16 Test sunglasses for correct fit and sew remaining halves of snap fasteners on the bag section.

17 Fold 15mm [⅝ in] satin bias binding in half around the edge of the case and tack in position, mitring corners as you go. It is best to hand-sew satin binding for the smoothest finish. Finally, remove all tacking.

THREADING THE SEWING MACHINE

New sewing machines incorporate the tension discs, thread guides and take-up lever inside the casing, eliminating various steps involved with threading older models. We include both because many older machines are still in use. If possible, consult the manufacturer's manual but here are general instructions for preparing the top thread on a sewing machine:

New style

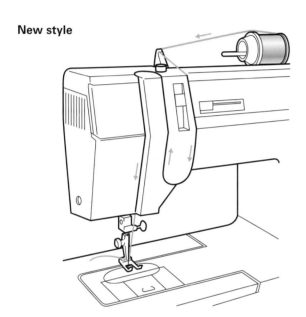

Old style

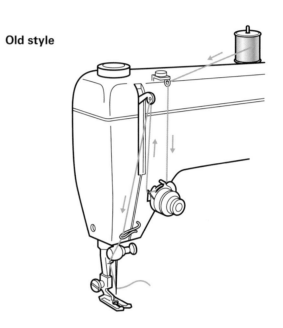

1 Lift the presser foot to release tension discs and allow thread to run easily

2 Raise needle as far as possible by turning the hand/balance wheel

3 Place a reel of thread on the spool pin and pull the free end into the first thread guide

4 On new-style machines, take thread around the auto tension channel and down to the thread guide just above the needle. On older models, thread around the tension dial and snap up through the tension wire

5 Older models also operate with a prominent take-up lever, pass the thread through the eye of this lever and then down to the thread guide just above the needle.

6 Now thread the needle. Be aware that some thread from front to back and some from left to right. Look for the groove above the eye where the thread runs during stitching. Finally, pull through a good working length of thread, about 15 cm [6 in].

Incorrect threading is probably responsible for more beginners' problems than any other factor. If you have no book of instructions, search for your make and model on the internet, where a huge range of manuals is available.

THE BOBBIN

The bobbin holds the lower thread on a sewing machine. It lies next to the needle plate, in a compartment with a sliding lid. Lower thread tension is controlled by a small screw that regulates the spring on the bobbin case. Some bobbins operate clockwise and others anticlockwise, once again, consult the manufacturer's manual.

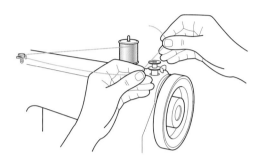

The bobbin is filled automatically from the winder on the machine, which ensures it is evenly wound under tension. Some bobbins can be filled in situ under the plate.

This type sits vertically in the bobbin chase and is released by a latch on the case. When replaced, the thread should slot under the spring with a tail of 10 cm [4 in].

The 'drop-in' type sits horizontally beneath the lid. There is usually an angled slot to pull the bobbin thread through.

THE IMPORTANCE OF TENSION

The machine stitch is formed by the top and lower threads interlocking in the fabric.

2 Between 4 and 5 on the dial is considered 'normal' tension. The threads meet in the centre of the fabric and the stitching appears the same on each side.

1 Top thread tension is governed by the tension dial, numbered 0-9. Behind it, the thread runs between two or three discs that are adjusted according to the dial.

3 Below 4, the tension discs loosen and the top thread runs more freely. The thread can then pass through both layers of fabric. This is only desirable if you want to create gathers by pulling up the bottom thread.

4 Above 5, the discs are screwed together more tightly and the reverse happens.

STITCH LENGTH

Stitch length is measured in millimetres from 1 to 6 and controlled by a dial or lever (p. 8). This activates the feed dogs, which in turn move fabric the required distance under the pressure foot.

Use the longest stitches (4-6 mm) for heavyweight fabrics, topstitching, and gathering. Medium length stitches (2.5-4 mm) are suitable for mid-weight fabrics. Fine fabrics may use a 2 mm stitch. A row of 1 mm stitches is difficult to unpick remember the value of tacking [basting] first.

STITCH WIDTH

Stitch width does not apply to straight stitching. The width control sets the 'swing' of the needle when working zigzag or other decorative stitches. The measurement is in millimetres and usually goes up to 6 mm.

MACHINING SPECIAL FABRICS

Sheer fabrics, like voile, organdie, batiste or chiffon look best with encased seams that don't detract from their delicate appearance. Remove selvedges [selvages] first to prevent puckering. The main problem lies with sheers being so thin and slippery to handle. Practice will help; take an offcut and run up a sample seam using the correct (new) needle and thread. The recommended needle size is 60-75 [8-11], with a fine cotton or polyester thread and a stitch length of 1.5-2 mm. If you have one, a single-hole needle plate helps to stabilize the fabric surface as the needle punches through. You can also try sewing with tissue paper under the fabric.

Denim looks tough enough in a finished garment but it frays readily and – like sheer fabrics – requires encased seams. Use a 75-90 [11-14] needle.

Velvets, due to the pile, can be as difficult as sheer fabrics and unpicking stitches from velvet leaves marks. Tacking should consist of short stitches with the occasional back stitch. On the machine, velvet takes a stitch length of 2-2.5 mm with a loosened thread tension, using a 75-90 [11-14] needle. Once again, practice on offcuts. If the velvet layers shift about, tack and pin firmly in the seam allowance before you begin. As you stitch, hold the bottom layer taut without dragging on the needle. Remove the pins as you go.

Knits must be handled with care while machining, it is all too easy to stretch them out of shape. Work at a gentle speed and remember that your seams need to give a little with the natural stretch of jersey fabric. Change your regular needle to a 75-90 [11-14] ballpoint that won't split the fibres as it sews. Use the stretch stitch on your machine, if you have it, or the tricot. Otherwise, try zigzag on the narrowest setting. Knits do not unravel so seam finishing is not necessary. However, you may feel than certain seams, shoulders and waists, for example, could benefit from being taped (p. 40).

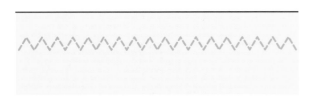

Stretching seam

Seam stretched in wear

MACHINING AN ENCASED SEAM

The sequence for machining a French seam is the same as it is for hand sewing (p. 22).

THE FLAT FELL SEAM

Sometimes called 'run and fell', this is another type of encased seam, widely used for tough-wearing casual clothes, skirts, trousers [pants], jeans and fabric bags. It is completely reversible with two visible rows of stitching on each side.

1 Pin wrong sides together and stitch with a 15 mm (⅝ in) seam allowance.

1.5 cm [⅝ in]

RS

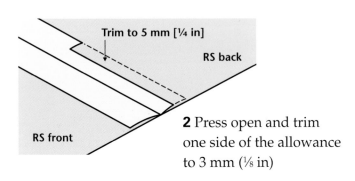

Trim to 5 mm [¼ in]

RS back

RS front

2 Press open and trim one side of the allowance to 3 mm (⅛ in)

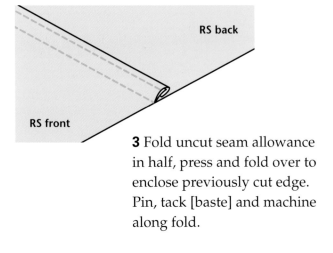

RS back

RS front

3 Fold uncut seam allowance in half, press and fold over to enclose previously cut edge. Pin, tack [baste] and machine along fold.

MACHINED SEAM FINISHES

The sequence for machining a bias binding is the same as it is for hand sewing, except that the final slip stitch (Step 3) may be replaced by machine stitching too. Here are some alternative seam finishes.

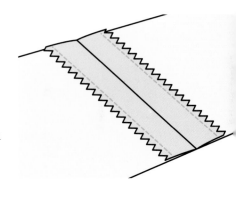

Edge stitched Stitch 3-6 mm [⅛-¼ in] from the raw edge on each side. Fold over on the stitch line and stitch close to the edge of the fold.

Stitched and pinked
A finish for close woven fabrics that prevents curling. Stitch 6 mm [¼ in] from the edge of each seam allowance. Trim close to stitching with pinking shears.

Zigzagged and trimmed Zigzag stitch down the edge of each allowance on the widest stitch setting but do not stitch over the edge. Trim close to stitching.

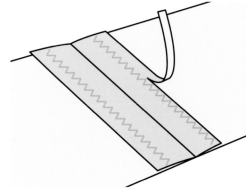

BINDING

There are two main types of binding tape, straight and bias. Tapes are manufactured in different materials, from heavy duty twill, through acrylic fibre, polycotton and satin, to nylon mesh. They also come in various widths. Straight tape is frequently used for ties and bag handles.

STRAIGHT TAPE

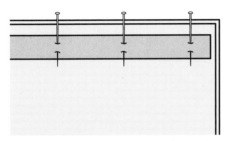

1 Straight tape reinforces seams where there may be too much tension on the sewing thread alone, such as on the shoulders and waistbands of lacy fabrics. The tape is pinned over the stitch line so that the stitching will go through three layers all together.

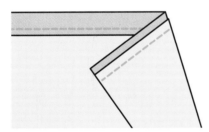

2 When the seam is done, the seam allowance is trimmed back close to the stitch line without cutting into the tape.

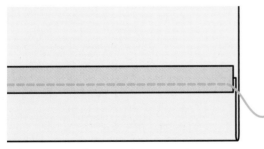

3 Straight tape is also used to turn hems where the fabric is very thick (eg woollen tweed) or fraying. Attach tape to the right side (RS) of the raw edge and use it as the hemming edge instead of the fabric itself.

BIAS BINDING

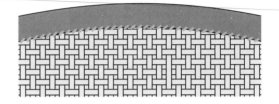

1 Bias binding, as its name implies, is manufactured on the bias (p. 12) and will follow the contours of any seam. It is used to encase fraying edges, particularly on thick fabrics and quilted items that cannot be neatened by turning. It also makes a decorative trim.

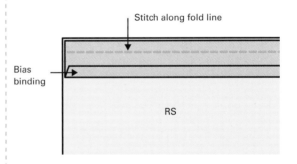

Stitch along fold line

Bias binding

RS

2 Press one half of the bias binding open, align with the raw edge of the fabric on the right side and stitch along the fold line of the binding (for speed, if possible use a sewing machine for this).

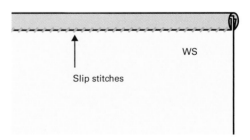

WS

Slip stitches

3 Fold binding over the raw edge to meet the previous line of stitches on the wrong side. Slip stitch along fold of binding.

BABY'S TOWELLING WRAP WITH HOOD
LEVEL **BEGINNER/INTERMEDIATE**

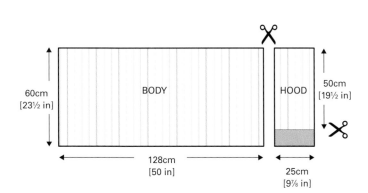

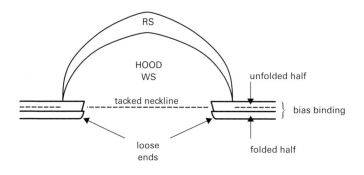

1 Cut off a strip 25 cm [10 in] wide for the hood. Cut strip once more to measure 50 cm [19½ in].

2 Trim one long edge of hood piece with bias binding (see method opposite).

3 Fold strip in half RS together, and join unbound edges to form hood 24 cm [9 in] square.

4 Fold main body piece in half and round off the corners.

5 RS together, match hood seam to middle of top edge of body section. Tack [baste] hood and body together firmly with 12mm [½ in] seam allowance.

6 Working on RS, unfold and attach binding to body section, starting on one side of hood leaving a 3.5 cm [1½ in] loose end. Tack and machine stitch bias binding right round to other side of hood, where you will leave another 3.5 cm [1½ in] loose end.

7 Turn loose ends back neatly on each side of hood. Align machine needle with existing stitch line and sew over one loose end, continue across hood and over loose end on other side. The hood is now properly attached and you can remove tacking thread.

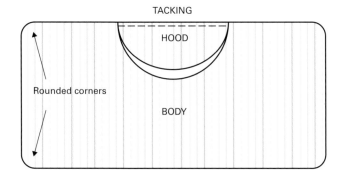

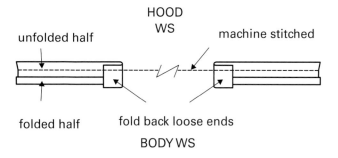

YOU WILL NEED
- Towelling fabric 155 x 60 cm [61 x 23.5 in]
- 5 metres [5½ yards] bias binding trim, 2.5 cm [1 in] wide
- 70 cm [27½ in] flat cotton tape for neckband and hanging loop
- Matching threads

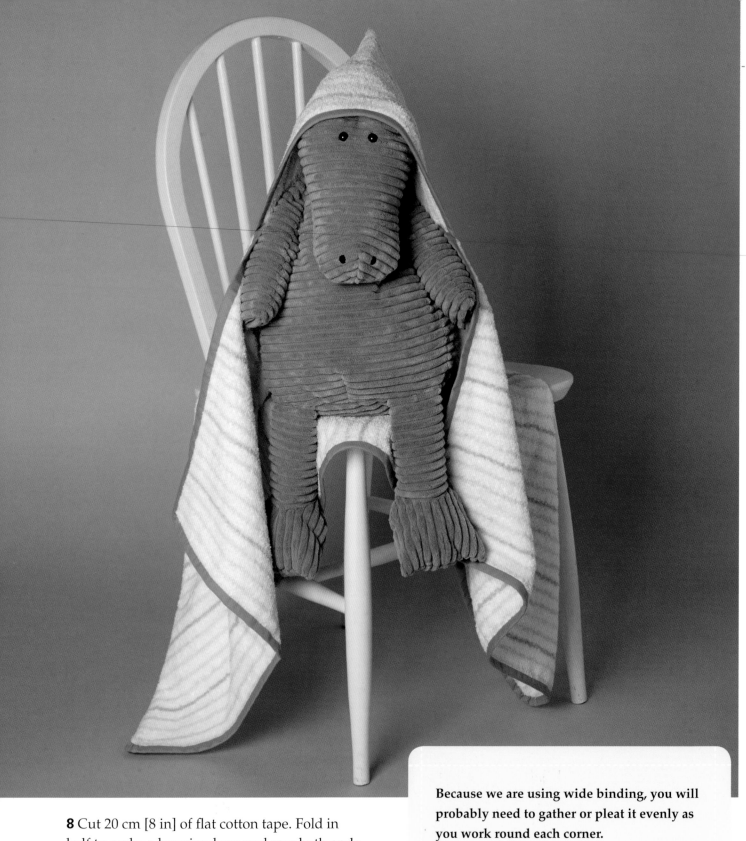

8 Cut 20 cm [8 in] of flat cotton tape. Fold in half to make a hanging loop and sew both ends securely into neck seam at centre back.

9 Press neck seam upwards and – tucking ends under as you go – hem stitch remaining 50 cm [19.5 in] of flat tape along both edges to cover the seam and create a smooth neckband.

Because we are using wide binding, you will probably need to gather or pleat it evenly as you work round each corner.

10 Finally, on WS, fold over and slip stitch (p. 15) remaining half of bias binding around body section.

POT HOLDER
LEVEL **BEGINNER**

You can machine or hand-sew this project. Do not use synthetic wadding, it is not heat resistant. Cotton wadding is safe.

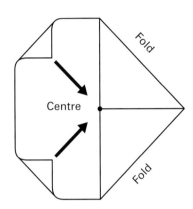

1 Cut the hems and selvedges from both face cloths and fold each corner to the centre, forming two new squares with sides measuring 23.5 cm [9 ¼ in].

YOU WILL NEED

- 2 new white towelling face cloths approximately 30 cm [12 in] square
- Patterned cotton fabric 46 x 23.5 cm [18 x 9¼ in]
- 102 cm [40 in] bias binding trim, 2.5 cm [1 in] wide
- 10 cm [4 in] flat cotton tape, 7mm [¼ in] wide for hanging loop
- Matching threads

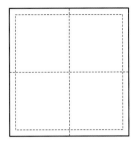

2 Put the two new squares together with folded surfaces facing and stitch first around the sides, then across the middle.

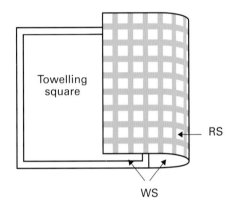

3 Lay the cotton fabric strip RS down and place the towelling square on one half of it before folding the remainder over to form a sandwich with the pattern RS outermost.

4 Using the zipper foot, stitch right around the sandwich about 7 mm [¼ in] from the edge. Trim layers level if necessary.

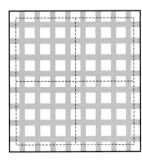

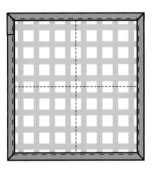

5 Fold the 2.5 cm [1 in] bias binding in half around the edge of the square and tack [baste] in position, mitring the corners neatly as you go. Fold the narrow flat tape to form a loop and include it in one corner.

6 You can either machine or hand-sew the binding. However, it takes practice on a machine to secure both sides of the tape at once. It can be less satisfactory than slip stitching either side to the base fabric (p. 15). Our example shows hand-sewing

PEG BAG
LEVEL BEGINNER/INTERMEDIATE

This is a very straightforward item to make. All edges are bias-bound so you will work right sides (RS) out throughout. The bias binding is top-stitched by machine, however it is advisable to tack [baste] it into position first because you will be sewing within quite a narrow margin.

1 Cut out the pattern pieces: (see pattern p. 119)
A Front section with opening
B Back section with curved notch for hanger hook
C Plain lining, half the depth of the bag, left open at base to insert hanger

2 Take C and double fold a total 1.5 cm [⅝ in] turning along the straight edge. Tack [baste] and machine stitch. Remove tacking [basting].

YOU WILL NEED

- Child's coat hanger or a plain wooden hanger, available from craft suppliers, cut down to 10 or 11 cm [4 or 4½ in] either side of the hook (smooth ends with sandpaper)
- Half a metre [yard] of patterned cotton fabric for bag
- 30 cm [12 in] square of plain cotton fabric for lining
- 1.3 metres bias binding trim, 2.5 cm [1 in] wide
- 70 cm [27½ in] bias binding trim in the same colour, 12 mm [½ in] wide
- Matching threads

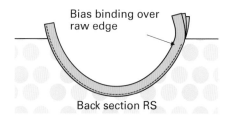

Bias binding over raw edge

Back section RS

3 Tack and machine stitch the 12 mm [½ in] binding around the curved notch on B. Leave 7 mm [¼ in] spare tape at either end and stitch along to the ends. Remove tacking.

4 Tack and machine stitch the 12 mm [½ in] binding around the opening on A. Leave 7 mm [¼ in] spare tape at either end and stitch along to the ends. Note that the hole is open at the top so the points overlap a little when the bag is assembled. Remove tacking.

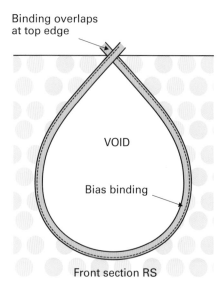

Binding overlaps at top edge

VOID

Bias binding

Front section RS

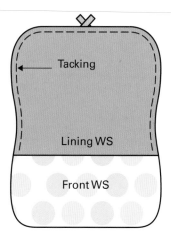

Tacking

Lining WS

Front WS

5 Lay A face down with the points overlapping, and C face down covering A with top edges aligned. Tack the two pieces together.

6 RS up, lay B on top of the other two and tack together around the edge.

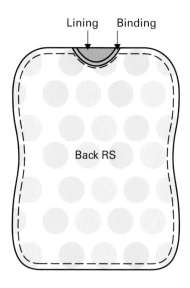

Lining   Binding

Back RS

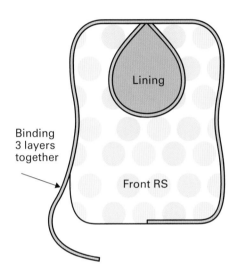

Lining

Binding
3 layers
together

Front RS

7 Bind all three layers with the 2.5 cm [1 in] wide tape, starting at the base of the bag. As before, tack before machining. At the top, trim the various ends of tape as necessary and enclose them in the wider binding. Continue and finish off at the base by turning the raw end under 12 mm [½ in].

8 Finally, insert the hanger upwards between lining C and back section B. The hook will come out through the bound notch.

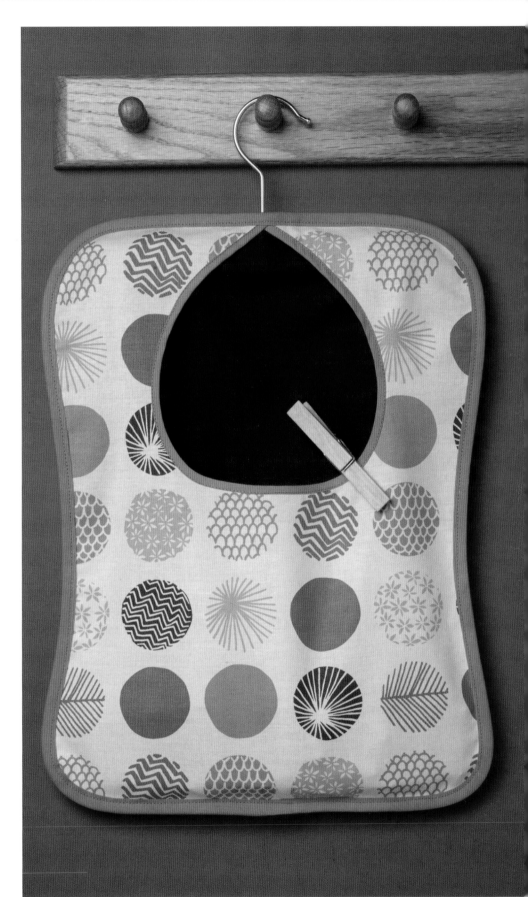

GATHERING AND PLEATING

Both gathers and pleats are designed to deal with the fullness of fabric.

GATHERS

Casings (p. 24) are an adjustable means of gathering – as is rufflette tape on curtains (pp. 48-49) – but we need to fix gathers permanently too, for example on a gathered skirt (pp. 62 and 75) or sleeve.

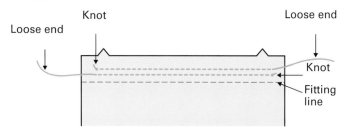

1 Within the seam allowance of 15 mm [⅝ in] sew two lines of evenly spaced running stitch in opposite directions. Start each with a strong knot and leave the far end loose.

2 The gathers will draw up when both loose ends are gently pulled at the same time. Wind each end around a pin to keep fabric to the desired width.

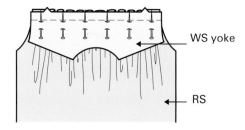

3 Lay the gathers out flat and adjust if necessary before pinning on the yoke or waistband and tacking [basting] ready for final stitching. This is the time to add straight tape reinforcement if required (p. 40).

PLEATS

Pleats regulate fullness in a more structured way than gathers. They need careful measurement and much preparation in terms of pinning and tacking [basting]. Have the steam iron ready because pleating demands that you press as you go.

1 A knife pleat is a simple fold in one direction only, either left or right. Pressing the pleats will set them but thicker fabrics are often edge stitched too, to keep a sharper outline.

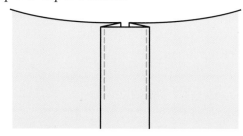

2 A box pleat is formed by two knife pleats facing opposite ways. On a skirt, these may be top stitched to smooth their shape around the hips

3 An inverted box pleat is created when the knife pleats point in towards each other. This is a common feature of pockets on military uniforms.

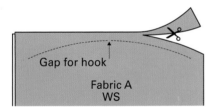

HANGING TIDY

LEVEL INTERMEDIATE/ADVANCED

We have made this version of the hanging tidy for gardeners to use in their greenhouses or sheds. Kitchens, bathrooms and wardrobes are other places where the tidy could be useful.

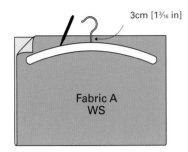

1 Right sides (RS) together, fold A in half and with a fabric marker trace the outline of the hanger onto the open end, 3 cm [1¼ in] from the top edge at its highest point.

2 Machine stitch the curved line leaving a small gap for the hook of the hanger. Trim to a curved seam allowance of 12 mm [½ in] and turn the backing RS out.

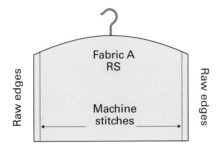

3 Insert the hanger and machine stitch a vertical seam from the tips of the hanger down to the base fold of A.

4 Trim the top edge of B, the pocket strip, with bias binding (p. 40).

5 Fold the strip into four box pleats (see opposite). The outer two are only half boxed and their plain sides will meet the raw edges of A with a seam allowance of 1.5 cm [⅝ in]. Select a long machine stitch along the bottom to hold the pleats.

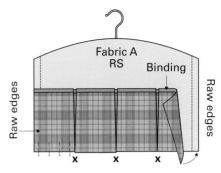

6 Pin the pleated strip to the base fold of A and release the box pleats at points 'X' by cutting into the machine stitching.

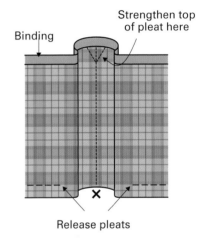

7 Open the box pleats just enough to take the width of the machine foot at the points marked 'X'. Attach B to A by stitching vertically from top to bottom in the centre back of each pleat. Reinforce the stitching where it joins the pocket tops. Press with a cloth.

8 Machine stitch across the base of B to close the box pleats once again.

9 With the remaining tape, bind around the tidy, enclosing both raw edges and the base.

10 Glue or stitch on an appliqué decoration if desired (pp. 26-29).

YOU WILL NEED

- A plain wooden hanger, available from craft suppliers
- 66 x 46 cm [26 x 18 in] of fabric A for the backing
- 74 x 16.5 cm [29⅛ x 6½ in] of fabric B for the pocket strip (quicker and more accurate to assemble if check [chequered] or striped)
- 2.5 metres bias binding trim, 12 mm or 2.5 cm [½ or 1 in] wide
- Scraps of felt for appliqué
- Matching threads
- Fabric marker
- PVA fabric glue

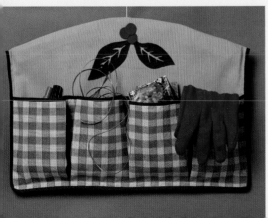

MAKING LINED CURTAINS
LEVEL INTERMEDIATE

A lined curtain is basically a cloth bag. The sides of the bag consist of two different materials, the curtain fabric and the lining. Linings are generally made of something like neutral-coloured cotton sateen but specialist fabrics are also available, such as black-out material or thermal lining.

YOU WILL NEED

• Curtain fabric, generally 2½ to 3 times the width of the window (or half the width in the case of a pair of curtains)
• Lining fabric, the same amount as the main fabric
• Curtain heading tape (Rufflette), 15 cm [6 in] longer than the curtain width
• Matching threads

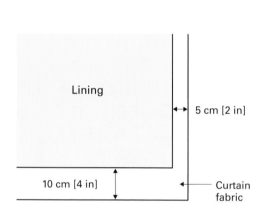

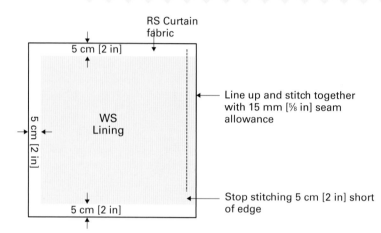

1 Having made sure you have your materials square on the grain (p. 12), cut the curtain fabric to the required size and cut the lining 10 cm [4 in] shorter and 10 cm [4 in] narrower than the curtain piece. Locate the centre widths at top and bottom of both pieces. Mark these four points by sewing a large cross stitch on each one in contrasting thread.

2 Place right sides (RS) together with the lining 5 cm [2 in] from both top and bottom of the curtain fabric. Align curtain and lining on one side, pin and stitch them together from top to bottom with 1.5 cm [⅝ in] seam allowance. Stop stitching 5 cm [2 in] short of the lower edge of the lining, where it will eventually be hemmed.

3 Pull the other side of the lining across to meet the remaining raw edge of the curtain. Pin and repeat Step 2. It is important to stitch from the top down in order to keep the curtain square. You now have a tube of fabric. Press both seams to prevent puckering.

4 Turn to RS and with lining uppermost, smooth the curtain flat and use the cross stitch markers to match the centre widths. The curtain fabric should show an equal margin either side of the lining. Tack [baste] the two layers together across the top of the lining. Shake the curtain out straight and iron down each side.

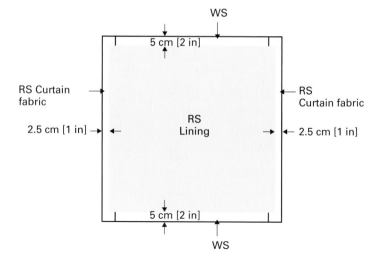

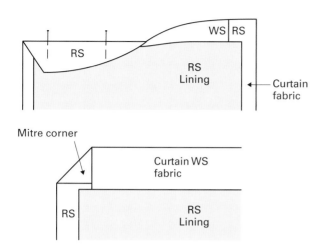

8 Tack [baste] and machine stitch the top edge of the tape to the curtain. Then stitch the lower edge. The tape will cover the raw edge of the curtain fabric.

9 Turn up, baste and stitch the hem on the lining.

10 Turn up, baste and stitch the hem on the curtain, which should hang below the edge of the lining. With heavy fabrics like velvet, some people like to let the curtains hang straight for a few days before hemming.

5 There should still be 5 cm [2 in] of curtain fabric showing above the lining. In preparation for the heading, first mitre the top corners by folding them in neatly at right angles. Next, fold the curtain fabric down to overlap the lining along the entire width. Pin and tack the head fold.

6 Before going any further, take time to check once more that the curtain is the correct length and width – and that the pattern is the right way up.

11 Tuck one half-bow of the gathering cords neatly inside the open end of the heading tape so they are completely hidden. Undo the bow on the other end and pull up the heading tape to the required width of the curtain. Even out the gathers before tying a fresh half-bow and tucking that one away like the first.

12 Attach the hooks, ready to hang the curtain.

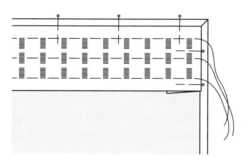

7 Pin the heading tape to the top of the curtain leaving a narrow strip of curtain fabric showing above it, roughly equal to the side margins. Leave 7.5 cm [3 in] extra tape hanging on either end. Unpick the gathering cords from both lengths of extra tape and tie each bunch in a half–bow (never cut these cords short because you won't be able to loosen the curtain or re-gather it after cleaning) . Trim the unstrung tape to 4 cm [1½ in], fold and pin under at each end.

ANATOMY OF A PAPER PATTERN

The front of the pattern shows a colour illustration of the garment but the back of the envelope gives you all the essential information.

Body measurements and size chart →

SIZES/TAILLES	8	10	12	14	16	18	20	22	24
Bust	31½	32½	34	36	38	40	42	44	46
Waist	24	25	26½	28	30	32	34	37	39
Hip	33½	34½	36	38	40	42	44	46	48
Poitrine	80	83	87	92	97	102	107	112	117
Taille	61	64	67	71	76	81	87	94	99
Hanches	85	88	92	97	102	107	112	117	122

Style number →

X852

EASY/FACILE

Garment description →

MISSES' TUNIC, SKIRT AND PANTS: Pullover tunic A has collar, front facing, pockets and unfinished edges. Slim fitting skirt B and pants C sit 1" below waist and have concealed elastic waistlines.

Notions → NOTIONS: Skirt B, Pants C: 1½ yds. of 1" Elastic.

Suggested fabrics → FABRICS: † Moderate Stretch Knits Only: Lightweight Wool Jersey, Cotton Knit and Interlock. Unsuitable for obvious diagonals, plaids or stripes. Use nap yardages/layouts for pile, shaded or one-way design fabrics. *with nap. **without nap.

Combinations: BB(8-10-12-14), F5(16-18-20-22-24)

TUNIQUE, JUPE ET PANTALON (J. femme):Tunique à passer par la tête A avec col, parementure devant, poches et bord sans finition. Jupe B et pantalon C droits à 2.5 cm au-dessous de la taille, avec ligne de taille élastiquée cachée.
MERCERIE: Jupe B, Pantalon C: 1.4 m d'Elastique (2.5 cm).
TISSUS: † Uniquement pour tricot à élasticité moyenne: Jersey de laine fin, Tricot de coton et interlock. Rayures/grandes diagonales/écossais ne conviennent pas. Compte non tenu des raccords de rayures/carreaux. *avec sens. **sans sens.

Séries: BB(8-10-12-14), F5(16-18-20-22-24)

SIZES	8	10	12	14	16	18	20	22	24
TUNIC A									
60"*	2	2⅛	2⅛	2⅛	2⅛	2⅛	2⅛	2⅛	2¼
SKIRT B									
60"*, 7/8 yd.									
PANTS C									
60"*	1¼	1¼	1¼	1¼	1⅜	1½	2⅛	2⅛	2¼

Meterage [yardage] required →

TAILLES	8	10	12	14	16	18	20	22	24
TUNIQUE A									
150 cm*	1.9	2.0	2.0	2.0	2.0	2.0	2.0	2.0	2.1
JUPE B									
150 cm*, 0.8 m									
PANTALON C									
150cm*	1.2	1.2	1.2	1.2	1.3	1.4	2.0	2.0	2.1

Finished garment measurements →

Metric equivalents →

Width, lower edge
	8	10	12	14	16	18	20	22	24
Tunic A	57½	58½	60	62	64	66	68	70	72
Skirt B	34	35	36½	38½	40½	42½	44½	46½	48½

Width, each leg
	8	10	12	14	16	18	20	22	24
Pants C	16½	17	17½	18	18½	19	19½	20	20½

Back length from base of your neck
	8	10	12	14	16	18	20	22	24
Tunic A	29¾	30	30¼	30½	30¾	31	31¼	31½	31¾

Back length from waist
Skirt B, 26"

Side length from waist
Pants C, 42"

Largeur, à l'ourlet
	8	10	12	14	16	18	20	22	24
Tunique A	146	149	152	157	163	168	173	178	183
Jupe B	87	89	93	98	103	108	113	118	123

Largeur, chaque jambe
	8	10	12	14	16	18	20	22	24
Pantalon C	42	43	45	46	47	48	50	51	52

Longueur – dos, votre nuque à l'ourlet
	8	10	12	14	16	18	20	22	24
Tunique A	76	76	77	78	78	79	80	80	81

Longueur – dos, taille à ourlet
Jupe B, 66 cm

Longueur – côté, taille à ourlet
Pantalon C, 107 cm

FRONT
DEVANT

A   A

FRONT
DEVANT

B   B

FRONT
DEVANT

C   C

Back view of garment →

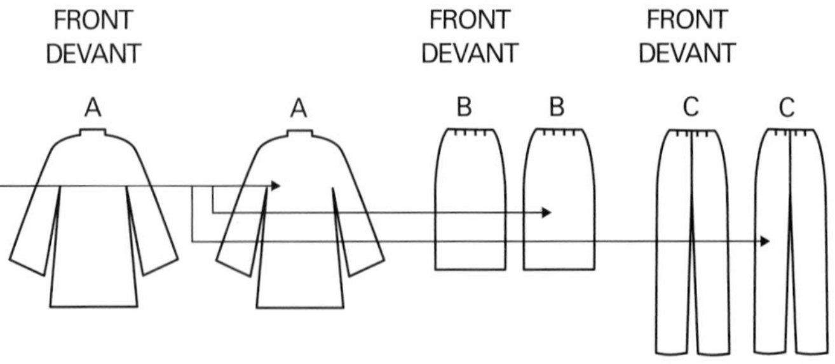

Inside the envelope you will find the printed pattern pieces together with the sheet of directions. This is a mini sewing tutorial, providing explanations of pattern markings, the cutting layout, fabric preparation, a glossary of terms, and step-by-step sewing instructions.

A typical cutting layout is shown below. Fabric is manufactured in standard widths of 91-115 cm [36-45 in] for dress cottons; 137-152 cm [52-60 in] for polyester, wool, fleece and furnishing fabrics. Different layouts are provided for each width and whether the fabric has a directional nap like velvet. Patterns for interfacings and linings are included. The information is generally full and precise.

With a check [plaid] fabric, wide stripes or a large repeat design you may not be able to cut out pattern pieces economically and need to buy extra fabric for matching seams and openings. This extra amount should be mentioned on the pattern, if not, ask the shop assistant for advice.

CUTTING LAYOUT

The paper pattern pieces are arranged and pinned along the lengthwise grain of the fabric (p. 12). The fabric is normally folded double but if a piece is to be cut from single thickness or on the crosswise grain it is clearly shown on the layout. The wrong side of the fabric is indicated by shading.

Pinning out is when you will take great care to match checks [plaids], stripes and any other important features of the fabric, such as shot silk or taffeta. A shot fabric has warp and weft [filling] in two different colours, so the fabric appears to change from one to the other at different angles.

If you need to mark your fabric – for example, to locate the position of darts or buttonholes – use tailor's chalk or a fabric marker pen (p. 6). Some have water soluble ink and some will simply fade after a day or two; always follow the maker's instructions for use, the pens are not usually recommended for 'dry clean only' fabric.

The notches on a paper pattern can either be cut out to stick up like a tab on the edge of the fabric or they can be cut the other way into the seam allowance.

S/L stands for Selvedge [Selvage]/Lisiere; F/P stands for Fold/Pliure. The numbers refer to the different pattern pieces.

NOTIONS

Notions are the extras required to make a garmnt, apart from the fabric itself. Typical notions consist of thread, fastenings and trimmings. Buy them at the same time as the main fabric to ensure a good match.

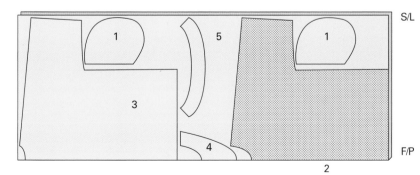

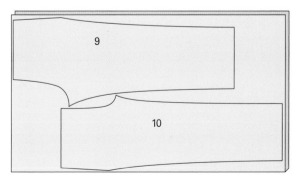

PAPER PATTERNS: TAKING MEASUREMENTS

In order to buy and use a paper pattern for clothing you must have the correct body measurements. The figures below show all the measurements you are likely to need.

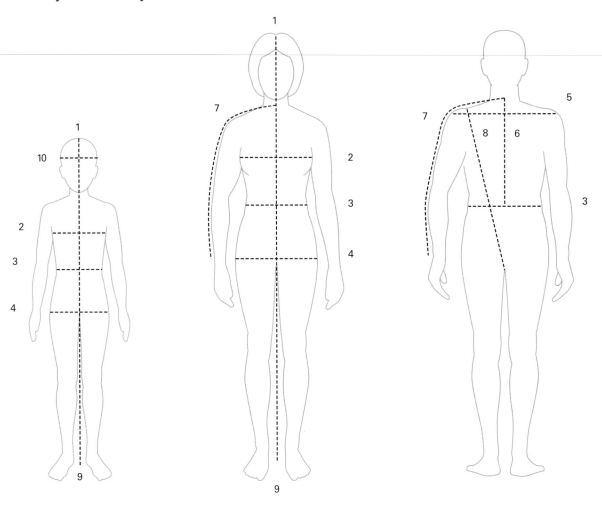

1 Height Stand flat against a wall and measure from top of head to floor

2 Bust or chest Measure around the fullest part

3 Waist Measure around the natural waistline, do not pull tight

4 Hips Measure around the fullest part

5 Shoulders Measure across back from point to point of shoulders

6 Back waist length Measure from nape of neck to waist

7 Sleeve length Measure from centre back neck, over point of shoulder and down slightly bent outer arm to wrist

8 Torso Measure from centre shoulder, under crotch, and back to shoulder

9 Inside leg Measure from crotch to instep on inner leg

10 Head Measure around widest part, across forehead

NIGHTDRESS
LEVEL INTERMEDIATE

A full-length nightdress with elasticated gathers makes up well in any lightweight cotton or silk-type fabric, or in a fine jersey knit. We used white broderie anglaise with a narrow pink lace trim. The measurements are for medium to large sizes; reduce accordingly for smaller sizes. Seam allowance is 12 mm [½ in] .

Squared pattern paper is available from needlecraft stores or online, for scaling patterns or drafting your own

1 Enlarge the pattern shapes onto a large sheet of squared pattern paper (p. 120). Pin the cut-out shapes to your fabric. Be sure to place both centre skirt sections on a fold.

2 Cut out the fabric pieces. Mark the positions of gathers on the front bodice with an air-erasable fabric pen.

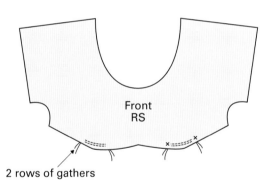

2 rows of gathers

3 Prepare two rows of gathers with running stitch (p. 14) between the Xs on the front bodice. Do not pull them up yet.

YOU WILL NEED
- Approximately 3.5 m [yards] of fabric, 115 cm [45 in] wide
- 4 metres [yards] bias binding tape, 2.5 cm [1 in] wide, for casings
- 2.5 metres [yards] lace trim for neckline and sleeves (optional)
- 2 metres [2¼ yards] of elastic, 7 mm [¼ in] wide
- Matching threads

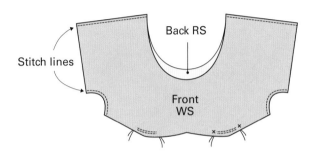

4 With right sides (RS) together, tacking [basting] and machine stitching, join the front and back bodice sections at the shoulders and sides. Overcast the raw edges together with a large zigzag stitch or press open and trim with pinking shears.

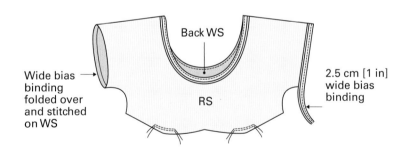

5 Bind the raw edges of the neck and sleeve holes with the bias tape that will also form the casings. Open one side of the tape, fold the raw end inwards, then tack [baste] and machine stitch it to the RS of the bodice with a narrow seam allowance. Flip the folded side of the tape over to the wrong side (WS) and stitch it down to complete the casing. Do not overlap the ends but turn the second end under, leaving a narrow opening between them for threading the elastic.

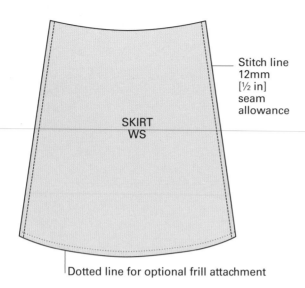

Stitch line 12mm [½ in] seam allowance

SKIRT WS

Dotted line for optional frill attachment

6 RS together, tacking and machine stitching, join the front and back skirt sections at the sides. Finish the seams as in Step 4.

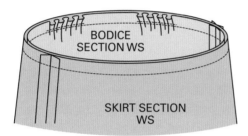

BODICE SECTION WS

SKIRT SECTION WS

7 RS together, pin the bodice to the skirt, matching the side seams. Draw up the two sets of gathers until the width of the bodice fits the skirt. Tack and machine stitch the bodice and skirt together.

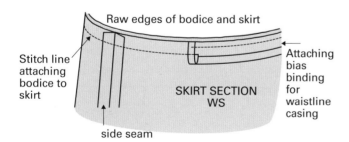

Raw edges of bodice and skirt

Stitch line attaching bodice to skirt

Attaching bias binding for waistline casing

SKIRT SECTION WS

side seam

8 Make a casing for the waist elastic by opening one side of the remaining bias tape, folding the raw end inwards, then tacking and machining it to the seam allowance shared by the bodice and skirt.

9 Turn the folded side of the tape up, tack and stitch it to the WS of the bodice to complete the casing. As in Step 5, do not overlap the ends but turn the second one under to leave a narrow opening for the elastic.

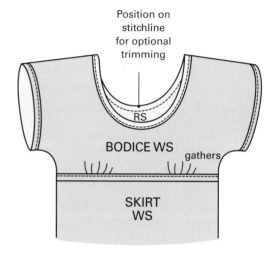

Position on stitchline for optional trimming

RS

BODICE WS

gathers

SKIRT WS

10 With the casings in place, it is time to add optional neck and sleeve trim on the RS, before inserting the elastic. Take care not to stitch across the casing itself.

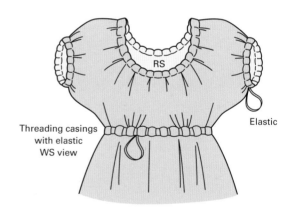

RS

Threading casings with elastic WS view

Elastic

11 Turn the nightdress inside out. Using a bodkin or large safety pin, thread the neckline and waist with 80 cm [32 in] of elastic each. Thread each sleeve with 35 cm [14 in]. Try the nightdress on and trim any excess elastic if necessary. Finally, join the ends by overlapping about 2.5 cm [1 in] and sewing firmly at the edges as well as in the middle.

12 You can either finish the skirt with an ordinary hem (p. 23), machine stitch a narrow turning, or – if you have enough fabric – add a frill to the lower edge.

RS view with trimmings added

13 As a final touch, cut a strip of self-fabric, approximately 65 x 4 cm [25 x 1½ in], join RS together with a 5 mm [³⁄₁₆ in] seam and turn RS out, as for a length of rouleau (p. 59). Press the strip flat, fold raw ends in and oversew neatly to close. Tie the strip in a bow and stitch to the front of the gathered waist.

MAKING DARTS

Darts give shape to flat fabric and enable it to fit over curved contours, for example on the bodice of a dress or the back of an armchair. They are marked by small dots on a paper pattern and are transferred to the fabric at the cutting-out stage with a fabric marker or tailor's chalk.

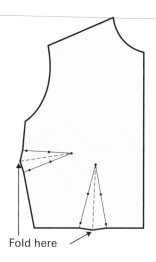

Fold here

1 Match pattern dots together by folding down the centre. You will see that the stitch line will eventually form a triangle.

2 Pin, tack [baste] and machine the dart to a sharp point by stitching past the edge of the fabric. Raise presser foot and cut threads, leaving sufficient length to finish neatly by hand.

3 Darts in lightweight fabrics do not usually need trimming, simply press the folded edge of the dart to one side without creasing the main fabric. Darts in thick fabric should be cut open on the fold and trimmed back before pressing.

SHAPED FACINGS

Facings are used to neaten the edges of necklines and armholes [armscyes] and are cut to the same shape and, most importantly, on the same grain or bias as the main garment. They can be stiffened a little with an interfacing if required, sewn or ironed on to the facing itself. It is easier to edge stitch or trim the outer edges of the facings with pinking shears before attaching.

1 The facing for a neckline, showing the joins between front and back sections, and the ends turned back where they are to meet the fastening on the main piece.

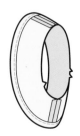

2 The facing for an armhole [armscye] prepared with edge stitching.

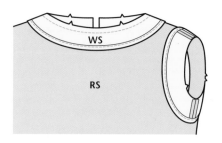

3 The facings attached to the main garment, ready for the curved seams to be clipped (p. 22) and turned right sides out.

ATTACHING SET-IN SLEEVES

There are many different styles of sleeve, for example (from left to right): raglan, dolman, bishop, puffed, tucked and tailored. Notice that neither dolman nor raglan styles have an over-shoulder seam, they are not 'set-in' like the others.

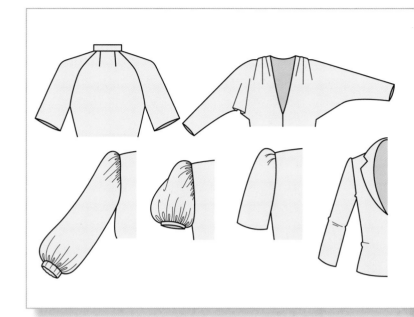

The set-in sleeve is joined to the main garment by a seam that goes all the way round the armhole [armscye]. Whether gathered or tailored, the set-in sleeve demands the most preparation by hand, although the final stage is usually machine sewn. The process begins with cutting out, it is immediately obvious that the sleeve head is larger than the armhole [armscye] it is intended for. However, it is the cut of the sleeve head that enables the arm to move freely.

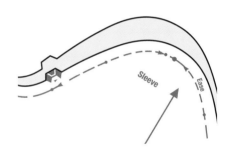

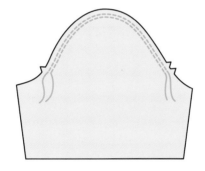

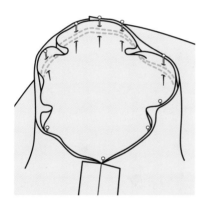

1 The sleeve pattern has notches that correspond to those on the armhole [armscye] of the main garment, and also markings to show the extent of the gathering line within the curve of the sleeve head.

2 Sew a double line of running stitches along the gathering line, leaving the thread ends free. Afterwards, join the sleeve seam, press it open and turn sleeve right side out.

3 Pin the head into the armhole [armscye] before pulling up to fit. Pull the gathers evenly and the head will smooth out. For a puffed sleeve rising above the shoulder seam, pull the outer line more than the inner one to make the sleeve head arch over.

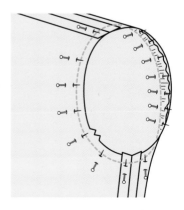

4 Distribute the gathers evenly, do not cut away any excess fabric yet. Tack [baste] firmly and remove the pins before trying the garment on. Now is the time for any alterations. A tailored sleeve should be smooth-fitting with no puckering on the right side. After final stitching, neaten armhole [armscye] by oversewing or binding.

OPENINGS AND FASTENINGS

The simplest type of opening is where the seam turnings are neatened with tape. Another type contains a placket (see right). This two-strip placket is neatly constructed from two pieces of fabric, one single and one folded double. It is an opening that could take a zip [zipper] (p. 71) just as easily as a row of buttons or a strip of hook-and-loop tape (Velcro see p. 71). Note the top-stitched reinforcement.

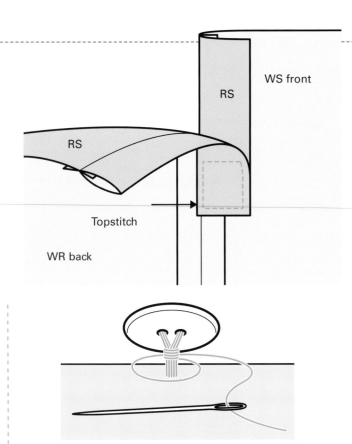

RS

WS front

RS

Topstitch

WR back

FASTENINGS

1 Use one or two hook and eye combinations to fasten a waistband, depending on the width. Waistbands take a lot of stress, so it's a good idea to stitch around the hook and eye attachments, with additional oversewing to prevent them loosening.

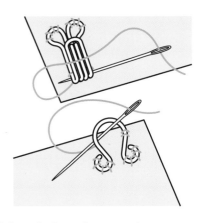

2 Use all four holes when sewing a snap fastener [snap] to the overlap. Don't allow stitches to show on the right side. Line up the position for the lower half by running your needle through the centre hole of the stud.

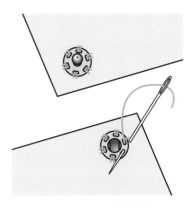

SEWING ON A COAT BUTTON

Use double sewing thread if you have no button thread. Do not sew coat buttons tight against the cloth but allow room for an extra layer when done up. Some buttons are manufactured with a shank but many are not. The thickness of two pins criss-crossed beneath the button will establish the shank's length and after a few stitches you can remove the pins and start to wind the thread around it. Finish with a few buttonhole stitches for extra strength.

SEWING A BUTTON LOOP

Loops make good alternative fastenings for clothes and bags, sewn on one edge to align with a toggle or button on the other. First anchor your thread with two small stitches on the spot. Measure the button width before looping across to a 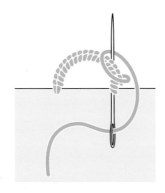 second fixing point. Continue looping to and fro several times then catch the strands together by buttonhole stitching around them in a solid line.

TRIMMINGS

FLAT RIBBON BOW

1 Loosely fold a length of wide ribbon into a rectangle with ends overlapping halfway down the longer side. Stitch the three layers together and lay a length of narrow ribbon across at right angles.

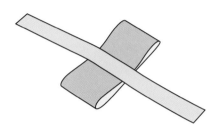

2 Turn both ribbons over and tie the narrow one in a knot that will pinch the wide ribbon into a bow shape.

3 Turn the ribbons right side (RS) up. Pull both ends of the narrow ribbon so they hang one side of the wide one. Trim level.

PIPING [CORDING]

Piping [cording] provides a smart external seam finish to clothes and home furnishings. The cord should be bought pre-shrunk; it comes in various thicknesses, use whichever is appropriate for your fabric. Piping needs to bend so it is encased in bias-cut strips (p. 12).

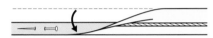

1 Pin the cord into the fabric and tack [baste], leaving a normal seam allowance.

2 Use a piping foot, although a zipper foot performs well too. Stitch as close as possible to the cord. A continuous strip of piping may be cut up and used as required.

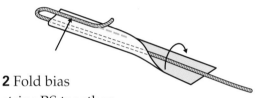

3 Alternatively, pin the piping in place and tack it to shape before machining. If turnings are bulky, layer them and cut off the excess to give neatly turned corners.

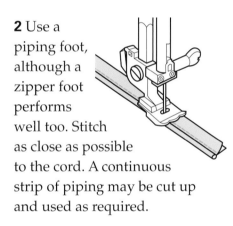

ROULEAU

1 Rouleau is constructed from bias strips (p. 12). It is used to make spaghetti straps; stitched-down designs on lapels and bodices; and wired trimmings for hats and bridal head-dresses.

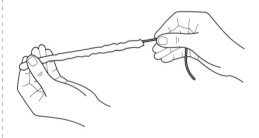

2 Fold bias strips RS together. Stretch the fabric slightly as you sew so it won't strain the thread later. Include a piece of string, longer than the tube, at the top of the seam and push the free end down inside. Finish stitching, without catching the string.

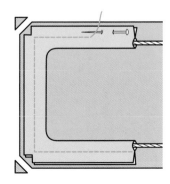

3 Trim the seam allowance to 3-7 mm [⅛ - ¼ in]. Pull on the string to turn the tube right side out. Pull slowly at first until you feel the fabric coming through. Alternatively, you could buy and use a metal rouleau turner with a latch hook (p. 64).

CHILD'S PARTY DRESS
LEVEL INTERMEDIATE/ADVANCED

The pattern for a simple high-waisted dress with full skirt is available from any pattern company and as a bonus, several variations are often given in one envelope. We chose plain short sleeves, added piping (cording) to the bodice and a contrasting hem to the underskirt but you can easily work your own ideas around this classic style.

1 Pin paper pattern to fabric according to cutting layout (pp. 50-51). Standard seam allowance is 1.5 cm [⅝ in].

2 Cut out fabric pieces. Include 'V' notches and mark positions of solid dots with a fabric pen.

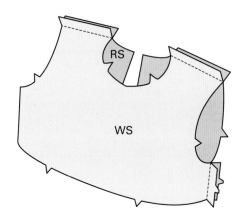

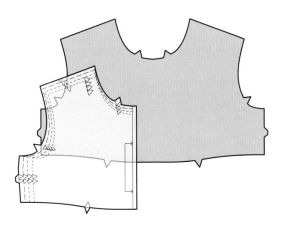

3 Stitch bodice front and back at shoulders and sides. Press seams open.

4 Prepare piping [cording] to go around base of bodice (p. 59). Tack [baste] and stitch into place on right side (RS) with 1.5 cm [⅝ in] seam allowance.

5 Repeat Step 3 for bodice lining.

6 Right sides (RS) together, pin, tack and stitch lining to bodice around neckline and back openings.

YOU WILL NEED

- A sewing machine, although gathers and hemming are done by hand
- A suitable paper pattern (pp. 46-48)
- Fabric: for precise quantity see your chosen pattern (3 different dress cottons were used here: tartan, plain black, and plain white for linings)
- Matching threads
- Notions (this dress used piping cord, black bias binding, and 3 x 1 cm [⅜ in] black buttons)

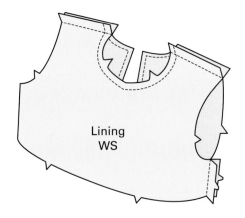

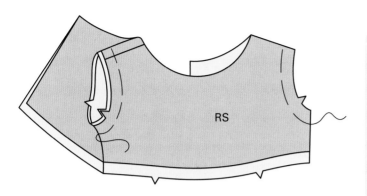

7 Clip neck curve (p. 22) and turn everything RS out. Press. Tack raw armhole [armscye] edges together.

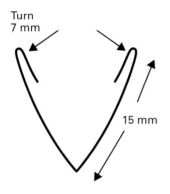

7 Clip neck curve (p. 22) and turn everything RS out. Press. Tack raw armhole [armscye] edges together.

8 Cut contrast trim for sleeve edges, 4.5 cm [1¾ in] wide. Fold in edges and press in half lengthways. Place raw sleeve edge inside centre fold. Pin, tack, and attach by hand or machine.

9 Set sleeves into ready-tacked armholes (p 57). Trim all three layers and bind armhole with tape.

10 RS together, stitch skirt back sections to within 10 cm [4 in] of the top and clip as shown. Press seam open. Turn under and slip-hem (p 23) the edges of the opening above the clip.

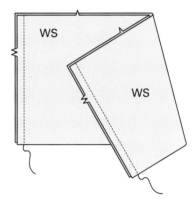

11 RS together, join front skirt to back at sides. Press seams.

12 Repeat Steps 10 and 11 for skirt lining.

13 Cut two hem bands, 19 cm [7½ in] deep, to go around skirt lining to form underskirt. Join bands at one end. Press seam open.

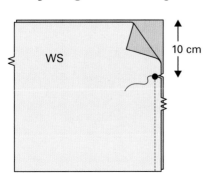

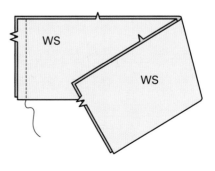

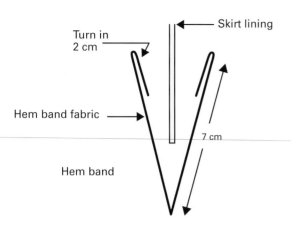

Skirt lining

Turn in
2 cm

Hem band fabric

Hem band

7 cm

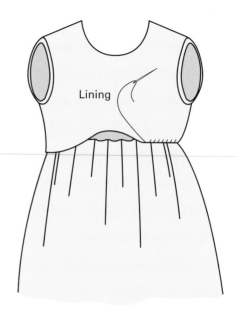

Lining

14 RS out, fold and press turnings and hem band lengthways. Place raw edge of skirt lining inside centre fold. Tack and machine-stitch band into place.

15 WS together, place underskirt inside main skirt. Align top edges, side seams and back openings. Stitch both layers together evenly around the top with two lines of running stitch.

16 Pull bodice lining aside. RS together, pin skirt, with underskirt, to main bodice just below piping. Match seams, pull up threads and even out gathers. Tack firmly and machine steadily with a long stitch, straightening skirt folds as you go. Within seam allowance, stitch round again at 7mm [¼ in] from first line. Trim close and press seam allowance upwards.

17 Conceal gathered seam by turning up lower edge of bodice lining and slip stitching on to underskirt.

18 Decide how much hem band you wish to show and hem overskirt to the correct depth.

19 Sew three buttons to back bodice and make three corresponding button loops (p. 71).

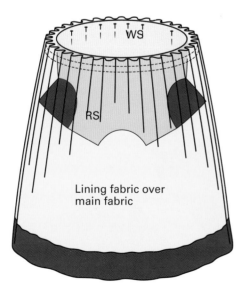

WS

RS

Lining fabric over
main fabric

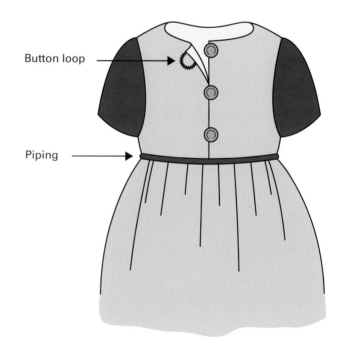

Button loop

Piping

CAMISOLE
LEVEL **INTERMEDIATE/ADVANCED**

See p. 120, each square on the pattern equals
2.3 cm [⅞ in] for an 82 cm [32 in] bust size.
However, if you alter the square value, you
can make this camisole larger or smaller. The
garment is ideally cut on the bias but it is
possible to make it on the straight grain too.

1 Fold, tack [baste] and stitch the bust darts from
side to point, and press (p. 56).

2 Place front and back sections wrong sides (WS)
together. Tack and machine the sides with 7 mm
[¼ in] seam allowance. If your fabric is slippery, put
a sheet of tissue paper between it and the needle
plate. (The paper tears away easily when finished.)
Trim seam if necessary and press to one side,
taking care to use the correct iron temperature.

3 Right sides (RS) facing, complete the encased
seams (p. 22) by sewing up the sides with 1cm
[⅜ in] seam allowance. Press both sides.

YOU WILL NEED

- 2 metres [yards] of
  lightweight fabric that drapes
  well, such as silk, crepe de
  Chine, flat crepe, polyester,
  or Tana lawn. Allow more for
  a self- lining if desired
- 1.25 metres [yards] matching
  bias binding,
  12 mm [½ in] wide, for facing
- 1.25 metres [yards] narrow
  trim such as picot braid or
  lace, for top edge. Allow
  more if trimming hemline
  as well
- Matching threads
- A loop turner for the rouleau
  straps (optional)
- Several sheets of tissue
  paper
- A sharp new machine
  needle, size 60/8 or 70/10.

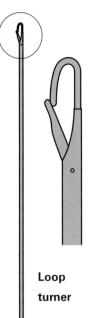

**Loop
turner**

4 RS together, fold each shoulder strap in half
lengthways and stitch with a seam allowance of
1 cm [⅜ in]. It is easier to machine a wider seam on
narrow straps and then cut off the excess. If you
have no loop turner, follow instructions on p. 59 for
attaching a length of thin string or strong crochet
cotton.

5 Trim seams down to 3 or 4 mm [about ⅛ in] and
pull the rouleau RS out, either with the string or
a metal loop turner. The loop turner goes into the
tube and out the other end. Hook on a little of the
fabric, then close the latch and pull gently until it
emerges RS out.

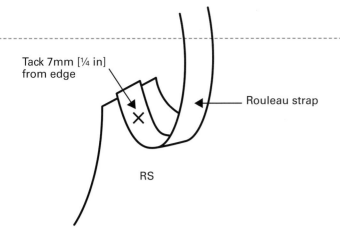

Tack 7mm [¼ in] from edge

Rouleau strap

RS

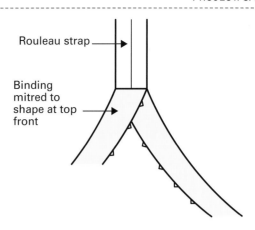

Rouleau strap

Binding mitred to shape at top front

6 At the points marked on the pattern, tack 7 mm [¼ in] of each strap to RS top front, aligning raw edges. Pin the other ends to RS back. Fit the camisole and adjust and trim straps if required. Tack 7 mm [¼ in] of each end to the back, as for the front.

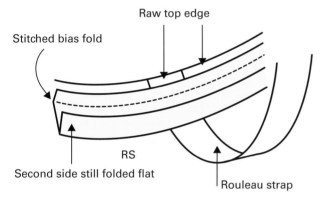

Raw top edge

Stitched bias fold

RS

Second side still folded flat

Rouleau strap

7 Press open one fold of the bias binding. Tack and machine stitch it around the top of the camisole. The four strap ends will eventually be secured and hidden inside the binding.

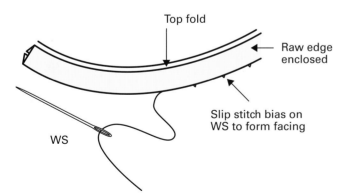

Top fold

Raw edge enclosed

Slip stitch bias on WS to form facing

WS

8 Turn the full width of the bias binding over to WS where it acts as facing material. The action of turning it over will also flip the ends of the straps to the WS. Slip stitch (p. 15) the free edge of the binding to the body of the camisole. The stitches will be concealed RS by braid or lace.

9 Mitre the bias binding neatly where the rouleau strap joins the body at top front. You can either fold the tape or cut and rejoin it, so long as the end of the strap is well secured underneath.

10 Turn up and tack a narrow hem in two stages to keep it even and make it easier to machine.

11 Add trim around the top. The alternative to a plain hem is to add a decorative edging of some kind. Here are two suggestions.

Shell edging Roll and tack a narrow double turning. Make a decorative hem with three running stitches followed by a vertical loop up over the edge. Pull tight to form the scallop. If necessary, make two vertical stitches, depending on fabric thickness.

Lace edging Tack a narrow turning, then pin and tack a length of lace – straight or gathered – behind the fold. Sew all three layers together with neat running stitch or use a straight machine stitch.

SURFACE DECORATION
Six popular embroidery stitches

DECORATED RUNNING STITCH

In embroidery, plain running stitch (p. 14) can be threaded or whipped with a second colour. Secure the embroidery cotton [floss] on the wrong side then bring the needle through.

1 Threading means sliding the needle up and down under the stitches without piercing the fabric until the end, when you fasten off on the wrong side.

2 Whipping means passing the needle under each stitch from top to bottom without piercing the fabric until the end, when you fasten off on the wrong side.

STEM STITCH

This useful stitch is a variation on the backstitch and can follow curves or straight lines.

1 Work slanted backstitches with the needle coming out a little above the previous stitch.

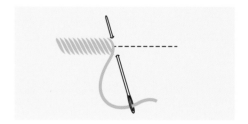

2 Create a thicker, more rope-like effect by inserting the needle at a sharper angle and increasing the number of strands of thread.

SATIN STITCH

Satin stitch probably originated in China, to show off their beautiful silk threads. Work the stitches very closely together to cover the fabric completely. Needle in and out at the same angle and keep to a sharply defined outline.

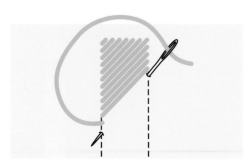 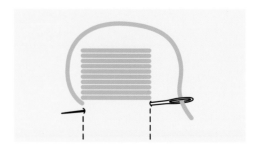

FRENCH KNOT

1 Wrap thread twice around the needle and pull gently to tighten coils towards the tip.

2 Insert needle, press thumb down to hold coils and pull thread gently but firmly through fabric, leaving a perfect knot on the surface.

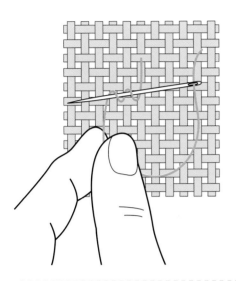

DAISY (LAZY DAISY) STITCH

A favourite stitch for depicting flowers and leaves, it can be worked to form a circle of as many petals as you wish.

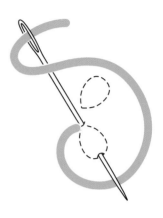

1 Begin as for chain stitch but work only one loop

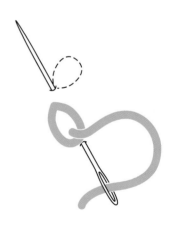

2 Instead of another link, make a very small tying stitch to hold the loop at its widest point. Bring the needle through again at the start of the next petal

CHAIN STITCH

A looped stitch used for both outlining and filling. It builds well with three or more strands of embroidery cotton [floss].

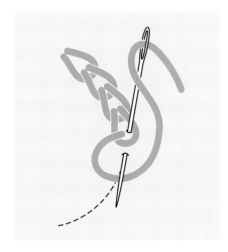

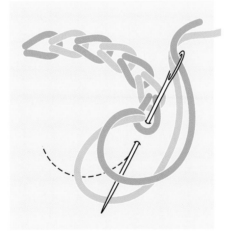

1 Bring the needle through and push in again beside the exit hole. Leave a loop on the right side and bring the needle up through it at a short distance below the starting point. Pull gently until you have formed a rounded link in the chain.

2 Thread your needle with two colours and work alternate chain stitches with them. Take care to keep the unused thread above the needle point.

APPLYING BEADS

Working with a milliner's needle, secure thread, bring needle through and thread on one bead. Insert needle back into or near the same hole. Advance one stitch on wrong side (WS) and bring needle through ready for next bead.

Thread two needles and secure both threads on WS. Bring first needle through and thread with desired number of beads. Using second needle, stitch over the first thread coming through the first bead, this is couching. Slide the second bead close to the first and repeat until all beads are in place.

For a bead fringe, tie first (anchor) bead onto thread and knot firmly. Add beads as desired, securing thread with two small stitches on the fabric edge before finishing off. Start a new strand in the same way, next to the first.

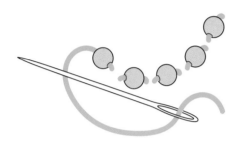

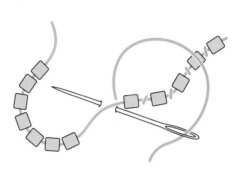

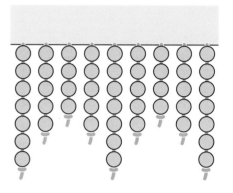

SEWING SEQUINS

Secure thread on wrong side (WS) and bring needle up through eye of first sequin. Back stitch over the right hand edge, come out on the left hand edge and back stitch down through the eye. Advance a stitch and repeat with next sequin.

To overlap, secure thread on WS and bring needle up through eye of first sequin. Needle in on left hand edge and up again at distance of half a sequin. Thread second sequin on and back stitch to edge of first one. Advance one stitch on WS and bring needle up again at distance of half a sequin. Each new sequin covers the eye of the previous one.

Secure thread on WS and bring needle up through eye of first sequin. Thread on one small bead before re-inserting needle through same eye. Pull firmly to bring bead in contact with sequin. Advance one stitch on WS and bring needle up through eye of next sequin.

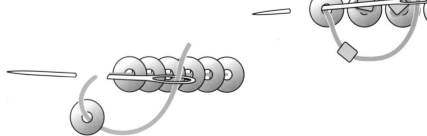

WRIST PINCUSHION

LEVEL **BEGINNER**

An ideal accessory when you are busy fitting clothes or soft furnishings.

YOU WILL NEED

- One strip felt 190 x 38 mm [7½ x 1½ in]
- Same size interfacing (canvas or thick Vilene)
- Two circles of felt 64 mm [2½ in] diameter
- Two circles of thin card 58 mm [2¼ in] diameter
- 9 mm [⅜ in] black elastic, 20 cm [8 in] long
- Matching threads
- Polyester fibre filling
- Scraps of felt, braid etc to decorate
- PVA fabric glue

1 Sew felt strip into a circle and turn right side (RS) out. With tiny blanket stitch (p 15), attach one felt circle to form the pincushion base.

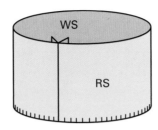

2 Use embroidery scissors to cut two slits in the base fabric 32 mm [1¼ in] apart, and just wide enough to take elastic. Repeat with one card circle.

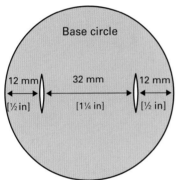

3 Place cut card on top of felt base, matching slits. Thread elastic through both, leaving ends hanging. Test elastic for wrist size and trim if necessary (it must go over your hand too!) Overlap ends of elastic by 2.5 cm [1 in] and sew together firmly (p 24).

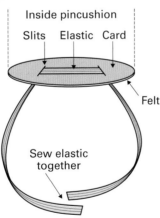

4 Pull elastic round gently until join lies inside cushion. Place uncut card circle over join.

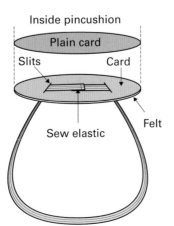

5 Line pincushion wall with the interfacing. Pack remaining space tightly with polyester filling.

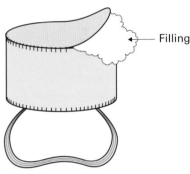

6 Using blanket stitch, attach second felt circle to top of pincushion, adding extra filling before closing.

7 Decorate the side with felt scraps and braid glued on with PVA. Or sew on sequins or tiny beads.

WAISTBANDS AND CUFFS

Waistbands need to be firm and are usually cut out in the warp direction (p. 12) parallel to the selvedge. They can be supported by a stiff tape like petersham, which remains visible on the inside of the band. A flat skirt or trouser hook is often incorporated into the overlapping end, with a bar to match on the other.

Alternatively, waistbands and cuffs can be strengthened internally with a material such as buckram or, more frequently, Vilene. Some interfacings iron on, which can save time but do check their machine washability.

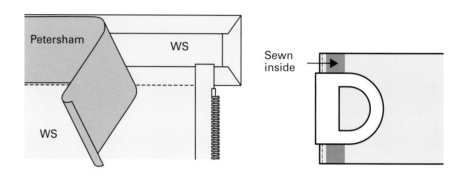

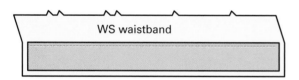

1 Fold waistband in half lengthwise and stitch interfacing into position against centre line.

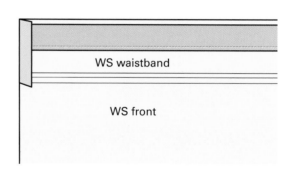

3 Trim and layer seam allowances to reduce bulk before they are encased.

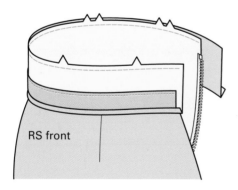

2 Match pattern notches, pin and tack [baste] right sides together and firmly stitch waistband to skirt (if possible use a sewing machine for this). Press up the narrow turning below the interfacing.

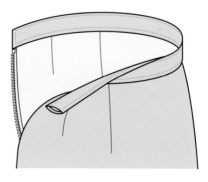

4 Fold waistband along edge of interfacing so that pressed-up edge meets main stitch line. Pin, tack and hem to finish.

INSERTING A ZIP FASTENER

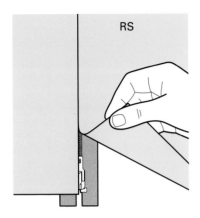

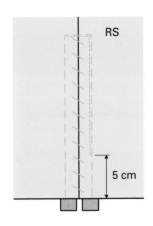

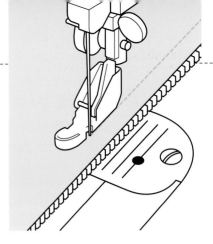

1 Set the zip [zipper] into the seam in the closed position. The fabric edges should meet at the centre and conceal the teeth.

2 Cross-tack [baste] the zip [zipper] with the ends of the zip tape turned down. Tack [baste] around the stitch line, passing about 2.5 cm [1 in] clear of the end of the zip teeth.

3 Start 5 cm [2 in] below the zip head in order to keep a straight line, and topstitch around the zip using the zipper foot to run close to the edge of the opening. Stop 5 cm [2 in] short of the zip head on the other side and, removing the cross-tacking [basting], slide the zip head down in order to complete the stitching both sides of the top.

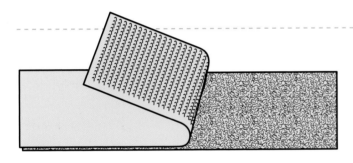

HOOK AND LOOP TAPE

The hook-and-loop system of fastening known as Velcro, is ideal for anybody who finds buttons and zip fasteners difficult to manage. Velcro tape can be trimmed to size without fraying and sewn in position as required on cuffs, waistbands and plackets. Take care to seal all Velcro surfaces before putting the garment into the washing machine because it can damage other fabrics by contact with its many tiny hooks.

MACHINING A BUTTONHOLE

1 Mark the desired position of the buttonhole(s) with a fabric marker. Using a zigzag machine foot, set the stitch selector and make a few stitches to form the 'bar' of the buttonhole before travelling steadily down the first side. Make the second bar at the bottom and then turn the fabric through 180 degrees to complete the other side.

2 Pierce the centre of the buttonhole with embroidery scissors or a seam ripper and cut open carefully from end to end without clipping into the bars.

A-LINE SKIRT
LEVEL INTERMEDIATE/ADVANCED

Three simple pattern pieces (see p. 121) make up this classic skirt, which has an inverted pleat in the front. The length can be adjusted to maxi, mid-calf or above-knee. Given measurements are for medium to large sizes; scale down accordingly for smaller waist and hips. Seam allowance is 1.5 cm [⅝ in] throughout.

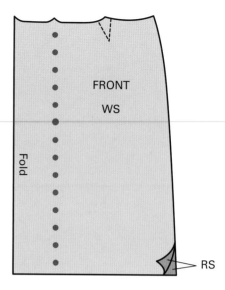

1 Enlarge the pattern shapes onto a large sheet of paper. Pin the cut-out shapes to your fabric. Be sure to place the centre front on a fold. In order to lengthen or shorten the skirt, cut across the paper pattern 45 cm [18 in] below the waist and pin the bottom section higher (overlapping the top section) or lower (creating a gap) as required.

2 Cut out the fabric pieces. Mark positions of darts and pleats with an air-erasable fabric pen.

3 Matching the notches on the waist, fold the front piece in half right sides (RS) together. Tack [baste] firmly in a straight line from the dot that marks the top of the pleat down to the lower (hem) edge. This temporarily holds together what will become the two front creases of the inverted pleat. Tack and machine stitch from the same dot upwards to the waist, forming a permanent central seam.

4 With wrong side (WS) uppermost, make an inverted box pleat by pressing down with your fingers to create symmetrical folds either side of the central notch on the waistline. Machine stitch across the pleat at the top to hold it in place. Turn to RS and check the pleat creases are straight on the grain (p. 12) before dry pressing with a cloth.

5 With RS facing, pin, tack and machine stitch the back pieces together, leaving space for the zip fastener to be inserted below the waistline. Press seam open, including turnings for the zip. Remove tacking [basting].

YOU WILL NEED

- Approximately 1.75 metres [yards] of fabric
- Strip of iron-on interfacing 90 x 10.5 cm [35 x 4⅛ in] for the waistband
- 2 metres [yards] binding tape 1.5 cm [⅝ in] wide for hem
- 20 cm [8 in] zip fastener
- One skirt hook and bar
- Matching threads

Stitchline

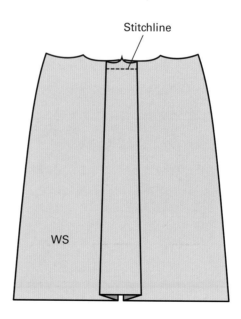
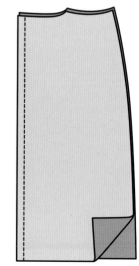

6 Tack and machine stitch the waist darts on WS of both front and back pieces (p. 56). Press darts towards the centre, front and back. Remove tacking.

7 Fit the zip fastener (p. 71). Remove tacking

8 RS together, join front and back sections by pinning, tacking and machine stitching the side seams. Remove tacking and press seams open.

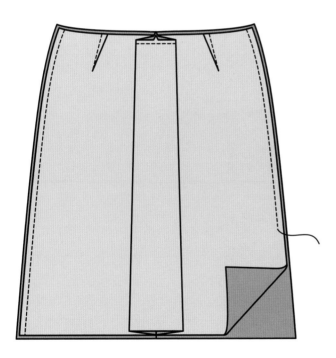

Squared pattern paper is available from needlecraft stores or online, for scaling patterns or drafting your own.

9 Cut interfacing to size and iron onto WS of waistband. WS together, fold waistband lengthwise and press.

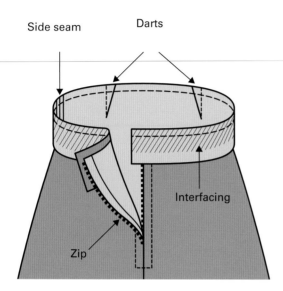

Side seam   Darts

Interfacing

Zip

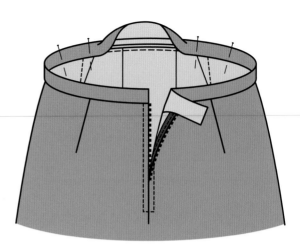

12 Pin the free half of the waistband to the inside. Turn raw edge under and hem stitch to the waistline seam, avoid stitching through to the RS of the skirt.

10 Unfold waistband once more and – RS together – pin, tack and stitch one half to the skirt top with the usual seam allowance. Press seam upwards. Trim seam allowances, grading layers if necessary

11 RS together, fold over each end of the waistband and stitch to close. Trim seams and corners and turn RS out, at the same time turning the whole waistband so RS of fabric shows on both sides. Press.

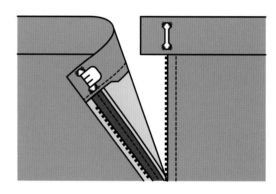

13 Attach the hook and bar skirt fastening. Remove all tacking.

14 You can either finish the skirt with an ordinary hem (p. 23), or – if the fabric is too thick to fold twice – machine stitch binding tape to RS of the raw edge (p. 40) and hem stitch the tape for a smoother finish.

> **You can reduce bulk on the central seam by removing the inner pleat layer to leave a wide, single layer seam allowance. To do this, cut along both inner creases from waist to 2.5 cm [1 in] above the dot that marks the pleat top, then across the pleat width. Back-stitch (p. 15) each side in a line from the central seam outwards, to hold the new pleat top in place. Sew the pleat to the seam allowance only, do not stitch through to the RS of the skirt.**

GATHERED SKIRT
LEVEL INTERMEDIATE

Featuring a plain waistband at the front and elastic at the back, this easy summer skirt also has one in-seam pocket. The seam allowance is 12 mm [½ in] throughout.

1 Scale up pattern (see p. 121) onto a large sheet of paper. Cut out waistband materials as instructed. Iron interfacing to both halves.

2 Scale up pattern and cut out pocket pieces as instructed p. 121.

3 Square up remaining fabric and cut two equal rectangles for front and back skirt sections.

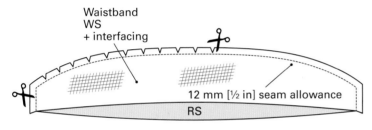

4 Right sides (RS) facing, sew waistband halves together leaving lower edges open. Snip the curve, trim corners, turn RS out and press.

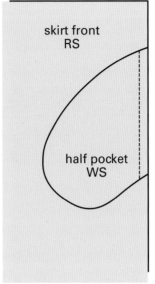
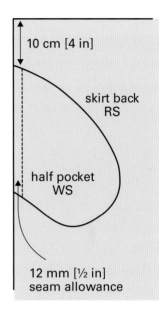

skirt front
RS

10 cm [4 in]

skirt back
RS

half pocket
WS

half pocket
WS

12 mm [½ in]
seam allowance

5 RS facing, tack [baste] and sew the pocket halves to corresponding front and back skirt sections, positioning them 10 cm [4 in] from the top. Press pockets outwards.

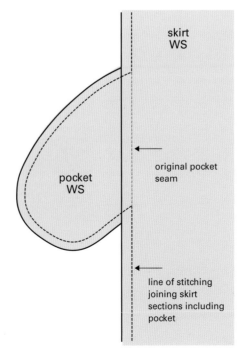

skirt
WS

pocket
WS

original pocket
seam

line of stitching
joining skirt
sections including
pocket

6 RS together, join front and back skirt sections, including pocket halves. Tack and sew starting 4 cm [1½ in] from the top edge. Press.

YOU WILL NEED

- Approximately 1¼ – ½ metres [yards] of dress cotton fabric, according to size required
- Strip of iron-on interfacing 40 x 20 cm [16 x 8 in]
- 1.5 metres [yards] bias binding for casing, 2.5 cm [1 in] wide
- Elastic 1 cm [⅜ in] wide, approximately 3.5 cm [1⅜ in] less in length than rear waist measurement
- Matching threads

7 Stitch straight down the remaining side without a pocket, also starting 4 cm [1½ in] from the top edge. Press seam.

8 Turn skirt RS out and press pocket opening to lie flat within the seam.

9 Unfold one side of the bias binding and, with raw ends tucked in, attach to RS top edge of back skirt section. Fold binding over to WS and top stitch lower edge onto skirt fabric, to form casing for the waist elastic.

10 Now trim the front skirt section level at its top edge with the back. Run two rows of gathering thread (p. 46) a little below the new trim line. Mark centre points on both waistband and front skirt with pins.

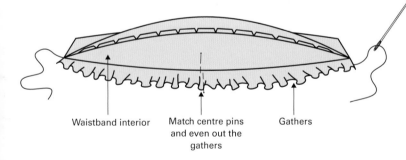

Waistband interior   Match centre pins   Gathers
                       and even out the
                       gathers

11 Draw up gathers and pin front half of waistband to gathered section, matching centre pin markers. Even out the gathers on either side.

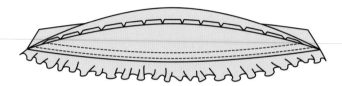

12 Tack front half of waistband to gathers with a double row of stitches, pulling tightly on the thread as you go. Check that the sides of the waistband appear level with the elastic casing.

13 Machine stitch the front sections of the waistband and skirt together. Remove tacking and press the gathers upwards.

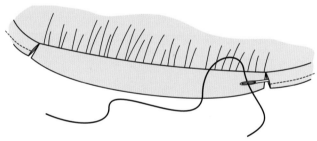

14 Close the rear half of the waistband with more tacking. Insert waist elastic through casing with a bodkin and stitch it firmly at both ends.

15 By hand, turn under the raw edge and hem the rear waistband along the lower edge, catching it down over the gathers so they are completely enclosed. Ladder stitch (p. 15) together the sides of the waistband and the open ends of the casing.

16 Finally, hem the skirt and press.

PADDED COAT HANGERS
LEVEL **BEGINNER/INTERMEDIATE**

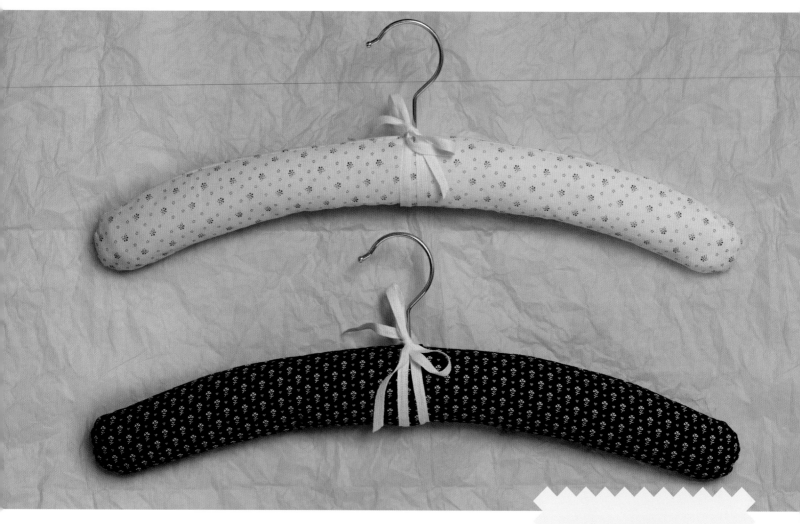

1 Fold the wadding [batting] into three lengthwise.

2 Fold in two widthways and with sharp pointed scissors make a small cut through all layers, halfway along the new fold.

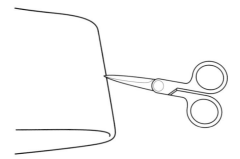

YOU WILL NEED

- A plain wooden coat hanger, available from craft suppliers – more durable than plastic and more stable than wire
- A quarter metre [yard] of close woven fabric, such as dress cotton [calico] or satin. You may need more or less according to the size of any pattern upon it
- Matching thread
- Lightweight synthetic wadding [batting] 45 x 30 cm [18 x 12 in]
- Glass-headed pins
- Narrow ribbon 7 mm x 75 cm [¼ x 30 in]

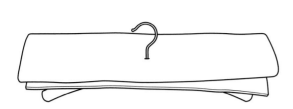

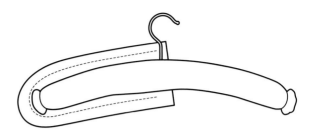

3 Push the hook through the cuts so the wadding lies on the arms of the hanger, folded area on top.

7 RS together, cut both layers in half vertically. Pin and tack [baste] the layers together leaving the vertical cuts open. Still WS out, slip the half-covers on over the wadding, adjusting seams where necessary for a smooth fit.

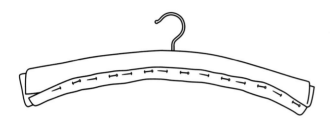

4 Curve the wadding around the arms so the cut edges are concealed and one fold overlaps the other. Pin along the upper fold.

8 Machine stitch each half and clip the curves (p 22).

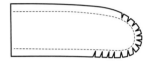

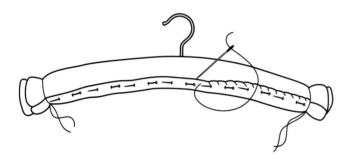

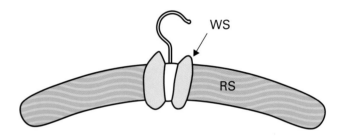

9 Turn both halves RS out and pull on firmly over the arms. Make sure upper and lower seams are in line. A knitting needle helps to smooth out any wrinkles between the fabric and the wadding.

5 Wrap strong thread – Xmas-cracker-style – tightly around the ends of the wadding. This cushions the tips of the arms. Oversew the pinned fold, pulling firmly so the curve of the hanger appears. Remove pins.

10 Stitch one half-cover around the hook, leaving the raw edges unturned. Repeat with the other half but this time fold in the raw edges and slip stitch the join. Tie narrow ribbon around the hanger for a neat finish.

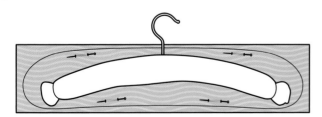

6 RS out, fold and pin your cover fabric in half. Draw round the hanger with a fabric marker. Allow a wide margin for the padding. Cut out the shape and make a template for more covers.

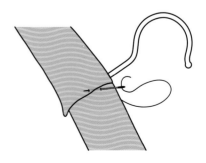

JEWELLERY ROLL
LEVEL **BEGINNER**

This roll can be made in any suitable fabric and used to protect and carry numerous other things, such as craft tools, kitchen utensils, art materials or make up.

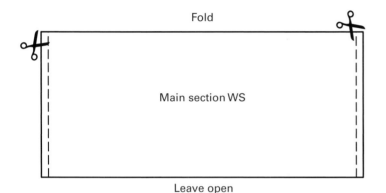

1 Fold main section in half lengthwise, right sides (RS) facing, and stitch sides together with 1.5 cm [⅝ in] seam allowance. Clip corners, turn RS out and press.

2 Overcast top edge and sides of pocket strip with 5mm [³⁄₁₆ in] zigzag stitch. At the top edge, fold 3.5 cm [1⅜ in] to wrong side (WS) and press.

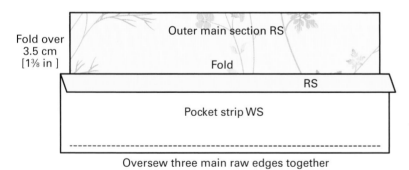

3 Lay main section flat with outer surface RS up. WS up, align pocket strip with main section at base. Tack and machine all three layers together at base with 1 cm [⅜ in] seam allowance. Finish seam with a wide zigzag stitch.

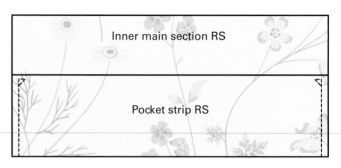

4 Flip pocket strip to inner side of main section and press lower fold. Turn under and tack sides level with main section. With top fold also turned inwards, topstitch sides of pocket strip to main section. Reinforce stitching where pocket joins backing.

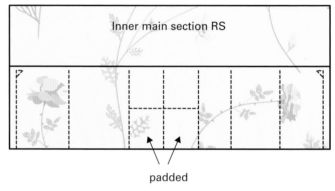

padded

5 Slide polyester wadding [batting] into the pocket strip, halfway along the total length. Tack and topstitch wadding into its own padded area (for pinning brooches and badges) with two small pockets above. Topstitch remaining divisions at intervals, as required.

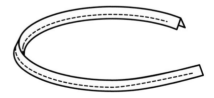

6 Make a tie by folding the 80 cm [32 in] strip in half lengthwise and sewing with 7mm [¼ in] seam allowance. Turn RS out, either with a piece of strong thread or a loop turner (p. 59 and p. 64). Turn raw ends in and oversew neatly. Press strip flat.

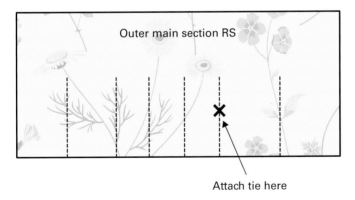

Outer main section RS

Attach tie here

7 Fold tie in the proportion of 4:3 and stitch that point to the outside of the roll. Attach firmly by machine, halfway along one of the existing stitch lines, as indicated by X.

8 Fold the top half down to cover the pocket openings. Roll and tie.

YOU WILL NEED

- Main section 64 x 67 cm [25¾ x 26¼ in] close-woven durable fabric, such as twill, canvas or furnishing fabric
- Pocket strip 22 x 67 cm [9⅜ x 26¼ in] of the same fabric
- Tie (minimum) 80 x 4 cm (32 x ½ in) of same fabric OR readymade tape 12mm [½ in] wide
- Polyester wadding [batting], 15 x 10 cm [6 x 4 in]
- Matching threads

COSMETICS HOLDALL
LEVEL **ADVANCED**

A tall, round drawstring bag, for carrying everything from an eye pencil to a small hairdryer when you take a trip. Unless otherwise stated, the seam allowance is 1.5 cm [⅝ in].

1 With a fabric marker, trace around the base circle onto the wrong sides (WS) of both outer fabric and scrap canvas, also on two layers of lining fabric.

2 Machine stitch over the circle drawn on the outer fabric *only*; this acts as a guide to assembling the base layers. Cut out all circles with a 1.5 cm [⅝ in] margin.

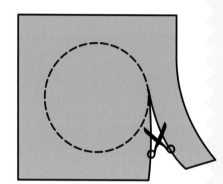

3 Cut two rectangles from the outer fabric.

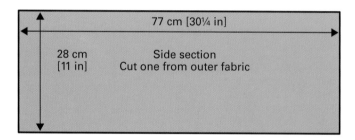

77 cm [30¼ in]

28 cm [11 in]

Side section
Cut one from outer fabric

77 cm [30¼ in]

18.5 cm [7¼ in]

Top section
Cut one from outer fabric

4 Assemble base, using the pre-stitched circle on the outer fabric to centre the 'sandwich'. Smooth each layer and pin edges.

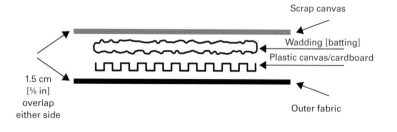

Scrap canvas

Wadding [batting]

Plastic canvas/cardboard

1.5 cm [⅝ in] overlap either side

Outer fabric

YOU WILL NEED

- A square metre [yard] of tough outer fabric like denim, twill or canvas
- A square metre [yard] of lining fabric like close woven cotton
- Heavy iron-on interfacing, 73.5 x 25 cm [29 x 9¾ in]
- 22 cm [8⅝ in] diameter base circle of plastic canvas or thick cardboard
- Two 22 cm [8⅝ in] diameter circles of synthetic wadding [batting]
- Square of scrap canvas, or similar fabric, approx. 30 cm [12 in]
- Piping [cording] cord 1.6 metres [2 yards]
- Drawstring cord 1 metre [yard]
- Bias tape to cover piping, 1.6 metres [2 yards] 2.5 cm [1 in] wide
- Bias tape for cord casing and fraying seams, 2.5 metres [3 yards] 2.5 cm [1 in] wide
- Elastic 76 cm [30 in] 12 mm [½ in] wide for interior straps
- Matching threads
- Fabric marker
- 1 bodkin or large safety pin for threading elastic

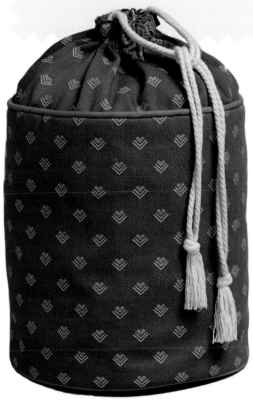

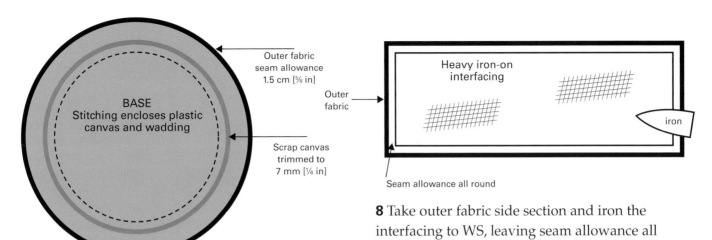

Outer fabric seam allowance 1.5 cm [⅝ in]

Outer fabric

BASE
Stitching encloses plastic canvas and wadding

Scrap canvas trimmed to 7 mm [¼ in]

Heavy iron-on interfacing

iron

Seam allowance all round

8 Take outer fabric side section and iron the interfacing to WS, leaving seam allowance all round.

5 Tack [baste] and machine layers together, using a zipper foot to stitch close against the canvas/cardboard edge. To reduce bulk, trim 1 cm [⅜ in] from the scrap canvas seam allowance but *not* from the outer fabric.

6 Make 155 cm [61 in] of piping [cording] to go round the holdall twice (p. 59).

7 Cut piping in half and hand-sew one length around the base on the right side (RS) of the outer fabric. Guided by the pre-stitched circle, sew firmly into the base seam allowance. Overlap piping ends as flat as possible into the seam allowance and trim no shorter than 2 cm [¾ in].

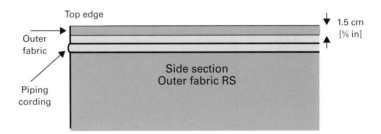

Top edge

Outer fabric

Piping cording

Side section Outer fabric RS

1.5 cm [⅝ in]

9 Machine stitch remaining piping to top edge RS of the side section.

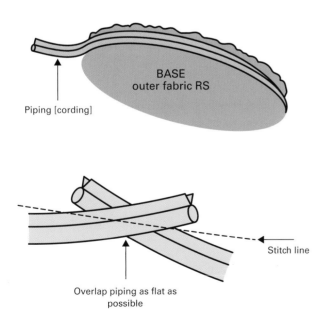

BASE outer fabric RS

Piping [cording]

Overlap piping as flat as possible

Stitch line

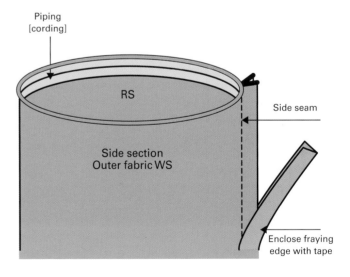

Piping [cording]

RS

Side seam

Side section Outer fabric WS

Enclose fraying edge with tape

10 RS together, join the side seam and overlap piping as in Step 7. Enclose seams with tape if there is a fraying problem.

11 Take outer fabric top section and RS together, join the side seam.

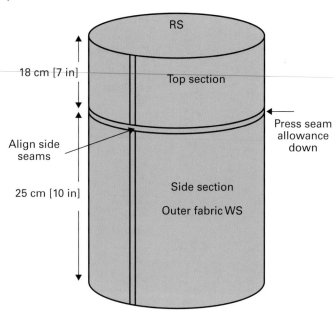

RS

18 cm [7 in]

Top section

Align side seams

Press seam allowance down

25 cm [10 in]

Side section

Outer fabric WS

12 Join top and side sections, stitching close to the piping, to create a cylinder 43 cm [17 in] tall. Trim seams level and press down away from the piping

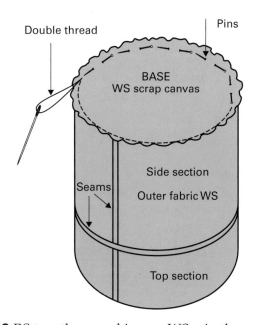

Double thread

Pins

BASE
WS scrap canvas

Seams

Side section

Outer fabric WS

Top section

13 RS together, working on WS, pin the assembled cylinder around the base. It should be a tight fit. Hand-sew in place with backstitch and double thread.

14 Place the remaining circle of wadding [batting] between the two circles of lining fabric. Top stitch around the circumference.

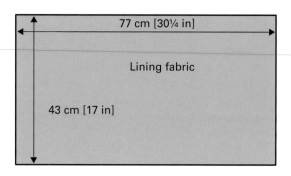

77 cm [30¼ in]

Lining fabric

43 cm [17 in]

15 Cut a rectangle from the lining fabric, 77 x 43 cm [30¼ x 17 in].

16 Cut a further three strips of 8 x 43 cm [3 x 17 in]. RS together fold each in half lengthways and make three strap casings with 7 mm [¼ in] seam allowance. Turn RS out and top stitch 7 mm [¼ in] down each side.

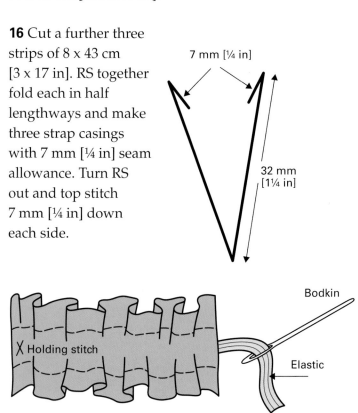

7 mm [¼ in]

32 mm [1¼ in]

Bodkin

Holding stitch

Elastic

17 Cut elastic into three lengths of 28, 25.5 and 23 cm [11, 10 and 9 in]. Sew some holding stitches at the start before threading elastic through the casing and stitching again at the other end.

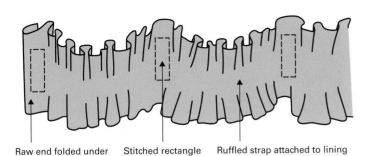

Raw end folded under   Stitched rectangle   Ruffled strap attached to lining

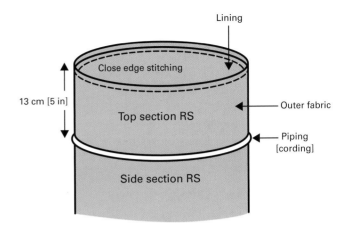

18 Spread lining fabric flat, RS up. Arrange ruffled straps as you wish. Fold raw ends under and attach to the lining with a stitched rectangle. Do the same to create three or four loops per strap. These are meant to hold various containers upright, so check the loops for stretchability and height. Also at this stage, add any pockets for smaller items.

19 RS together, join the side seam of the lining and press.

20 Tack [baste] the padded base inside the lining fabric (similar to Step 13). Machine stitch to complete the lining.

21 With both outer fabric and lining WS out, join them by pinning bases together and hand-sewing around the base seam. Turn outer fabric RS out to enclose the lining.

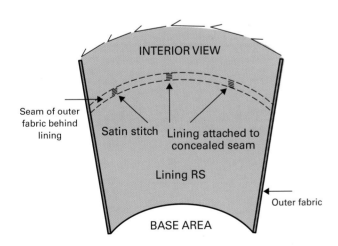

INTERIOR VIEW

Seam of outer fabric behind lining

Satin stitch   Lining attached to concealed seam

Lining RS

Outer fabric

BASE AREA

22 Pull the sides of the lining up straight and, on the inside of the holdall, with a few neat satin stitches (p. 66), attach the lining at intervals around the seam that joins the side and top sections of the outer fabric.

23 Align the top edges of outer fabric and lining. Fold in towards each other until the outer top section measures 13 cm [5 in] deep. Tack and machine stitch as close to the edge as you can with thread matching the outer fabric.

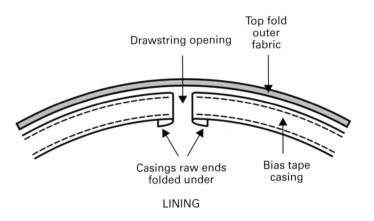

Drawstring opening   Top fold outer fabric

Casings raw ends folded under   Bias tape casing

LINING

24 Prepare two lengths of 2.5 cm [1 in] bias tape for the drawstring casings. Both lengths are sewn with openings on either side of the holdall (see also p. 25). Load the machine with top thread to match the casing tape, and the bobbin to match the outer cover. Machine stitch both edges of the casing.

25 Thread casing with two-way cord loops (see p. 25).

RETRO KNITTING BAG
LEVEL BEGINNER/INTERMEDIATE

A fully lined work bag with generous inner pockets – so much better than a plastic carrier for keeping your knitting or needlework.

1 Prepare pieces from both outer fabric A and lining B (see p. 121).

2 Take the two pocket sections cut from fabric B. Double fold 1.5 cm [⅝ in] and topstitch one short side on each section for the pocket opening. On the wrong side (WS) of each, fold in 1 cm [⅜ in] around the other three sides and press firmly.

3 Tack [baste] and topstitch the pockets to the main lining with a 5 mm [³⁄₁₆ in] margin. Centre them on the width of the fabric and position 17 cm [6½ in] apart at the base. Reinforce the stitching where it joins the pocket tops by reverse stitching at a slight angle. The pockets may be subdivided by more topstitching. Create narrow

compartments – just 2.5 cm [1 in] wide – to take spare knitting needles. Remove tacking.

4 RS facing, stitch the main sections of bag and lining together on each side with a seam allowance of 1.5 cm [⅝ in]. Turn RS out and press from the lining side.

5 Repeat Step 4 with the two side panels, this time including the base seam. Clip corners and turn RS out. Press from the lining side.

6 Continuing with the side panels, fold inwards the top 1 cm [⅜ in] of both main fabric and lining, tack and topstitch the layers together 7 mm [¼ in] from the edge.

LINING
RS

Cut from lining fabric 2 pockets approx 25.5 x 23 cm [10 x 9 in]

BASE AREA

Topstitch pockets to lining

MAIN FABRIC
WS

lining RS

Stitch sides together

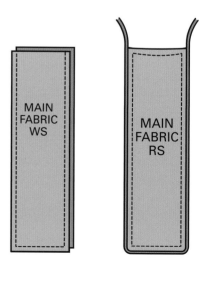

MAIN FABRIC WS

MAIN FABRIC RS

YOU WILL NEED
- A pair of acrylic handles
- Outer fabric A 91.5 x 41 cm [36 x 16 in], babycord or pre-quilted cotton
- Two side panels A 35.5 x 12.5 cm [14 x 5 in]
- Lining fabric B 91.5 x 41 cm [36 x 16 in], dress cotton
- Two side panels B 35.5 x 12.5 cm [14 x 5 in]
- Two inner pockets B 25.5 x 28 cm [10 x 11 in]
- Matching threads

7 WS together, fold the main bag section in half and mark the lower fold on either side with a pin or tag of thread. WS together, fold one side panel in half lengthways and mark the fold on the lower edge. Keeping WS together, match both halfway points and begin tacking along the base, then up towards the top of the panel, and fasten off. Go back to the halfway point and tack up the other side of the panel in the same way. Repeat everything with the second panel on the opposite side. When tacking is complete, set the machine to a long stitch and topstitch 1 cm [⅜ in] from the edge. Reinforce by hand oversewing where the main bag section and the panels meet. Remove tacking.

8 Take the remaining raw edges at the top of the main bag section and trim level if necessary. One side at a time, fold 1 cm [⅜ in] of both fabric and lining in towards each other. Tack and topstitch the layers together by machine, 7 mm [¼ in] from the edge. Remove tacking and press from the lining side.

9 The acrylic handles have slots for attaching the fabric. Run a single gathering thread along the top edge of each side of the bag (p. 46). Draw up until the width of the fabric matches the slot. Hold by oversewing once or twice with the end of the gathering thread.

10 Feed the edges of the fabric through the slots from the outside in. Distribute the gathers evenly and pin the edges down to the lining fabric. With matching double thread, begin hand sewing in a line immediately below the handles. Stab stitch through all the layers, using a large back stitch (p. 14) and pulling firmly as you go. Finish off securely.

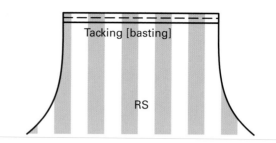

Tacking [basting]

RS

APRON
LEVEL BEGINNER

A practical, full length apron with a large double pocket – ideal for cooks, gardeners or crafts people.

1 Scale up the pattern (see p. 122) onto a large sheet of paper. Pin cut-out paper to fabric, remembering to place the centre line of the apron on a fold. Cut out both apron and pocket.

2 Turn and tack [baste] 6 mm [¼ in] to the wrong side (WS) of both armholes. Turn and tack a further 1 cm [⅜ in]. Press curve.

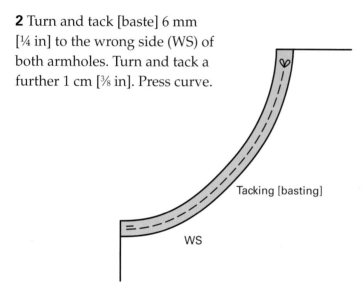

Tacking [basting]

WS

3 Turn 6 mm [¼ in] of bib top to the right side (RS) and tack [baste].

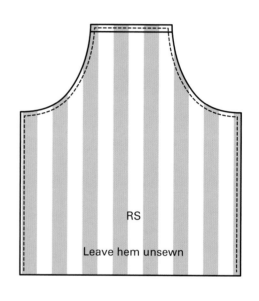

RS

Leave hem unsewn

4 Tack side hems, turning 6 mm [¼ in] then 12 mm [½ in] before machine stitching right round the apron, except for the bottom hem. Remove all tacking.

5 Cut two lengths of tape, 30 cm [12 in] for bib band and 57 cm [22½ in] for neck strap. Enclose raw ends of neck strap inside turned ends of the bib band, which should be the same width as the bib top. Tack the ends before machine stitching in an 'X'.

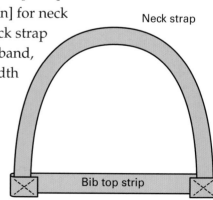

Neck strap

Bib top strip

YOU WILL NEED

- One metre [yard] of pre-shrunk cotton fabric, twill or light canvas
- 51 x 26 cm [20 x 10 in] of plain or contrasting fabric for the pocket
- 120 cm [3 yards] of herringbone tape 2.5 cm [1 in] wide OR make strips from matching pocket fabric
- Matching threads

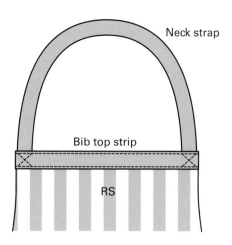

Neck strap

Bib top strip

RS

6 Tack and machine assembled bib band in position on RS, topstitching along both edges of the tape and concealing raw edge of bib.

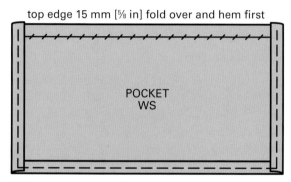

top edge 15 mm [⅝ in] fold over and hem first

POCKET
WS

Fold over 15 mm [⅝ in] and tack on other three sides

7 Turn a narrow hem along the top edge of pocket fabric. On WS, fold over and tack 15 mm [⅝ in] around the other three sides. Press on WS.

8 Pin centre width of pocket to centre width of apron, 39 cm [15 in] from the top of the bib (adjust for preference). Topstitch sides and centre line of pocket to the apron fabric before closing along the base.

9 Cut remaining tape in half and attach to WS of apron at waist level, folding raw ends under before machine stitching in an 'X'. Oversew free ends to prevent fraying

10 Finally, turn 6 mm [¼ in] then 19 mm [¾ in] and tack before stitching the lower hem.

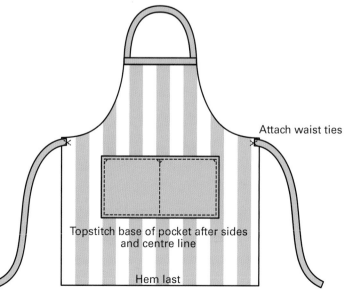

Attach waist ties

Topstitch base of pocket after sides and centre line

Hem last

FOUR EGG COSIES
LEVEL BEGINNER

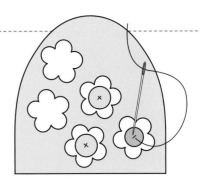

3 It's easier to add features and decorations to separate halves before stitching them together. Attach daisies by neat cross stitches, petals first, then coloured centres on top. Finally, join the two halves with neat blanket stitch around the curve.

4 Chick's big round eyes are based on two sizes of coin.

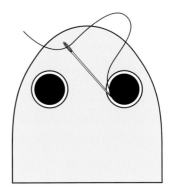

5 Best to stitch right round larger features.

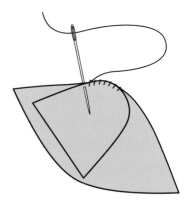

6 Beak templates. Join both parts with neat blanket stitch.

YOU WILL NEED

- A 30 cm [12 in] felt square in your chosen base colour for each cosy, alternatively two 15 cm [6 in] squares of different colours
- Smaller pieces of other colours, as required
- Matching threads
- Synthetic filling for Chick's beak
- 10 cm [3 in] narrow gold braid for Guardsman
- Sequins for Guardsman and Princess
- Fabric marker pen
- Small pointed scissors
- PVA fabric glue

1 Copy basic shape onto paper, cut out and use as template for all cosies. Trace around shape with fabric marker onto felt. Template includes 4 mm [⅛ in] seam allowance. If your egg cup is wider or taller than average, adjust template accordingly. For all egg cosy templates see pp. 124–125)

2 Templates for the Daisy cosy, petals are white while centres are different colours. Cut five flowers for each half.

When machine stitching two identical shapes together, mark out, pin and stitch both layers in whole felt first before cutting out around the stitch line with a 4 mm [⅛ in] margin.

7 Beak ready for filling.

8 Preparing to sew beak onto Chick, it must be centred and near the eyes.

9 Pin and sew padded beak. Start by stitching corners to hold in position. Use running stitch to attach rest of beak to face.

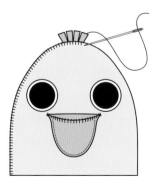

10 Join both halves using blanket stitch. Add tuft of orange felt at top of curve, sandwiched between layers with tiny running stitches.

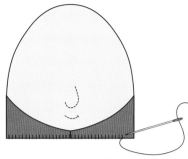

11 Can't see much face under a Guardsman's busby. Backstitch nose and mouth in one shade of embroidery silk [floss]. Blanket stitch red tunic at base.

12 Busby and back half attached simultaneously, using red and black thread.

13 Glue narrow gold braid and two sequins to red tunic.

14 Templates for Princess's dress, cut from two or three colours.

15 Templates for Princess's hair, eyes and crown, cut from two or three colours.

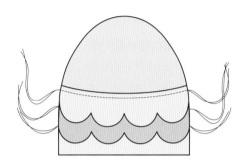

16 Machine or handstitch dress. Overlap each tier, starting at the straight edge.

17 Sew eyes to face using hair as guide to placing. Do not attach hair yet. Nose embroidered with two french knots and mouth backstitched with pale pink embroidery silk [floss]. Princess's hair and back half sewn together simultaneously, using brown and flesh thread. Do not sew dress at sides, hide stitches under tiers.

18 Finally, glue crown and sequins into place.

INTRODUCING PATCHWORK

Choose something small for a first attempt. Place mats, cushion covers, bags and cot quilts are all good starter projects.

TEMPLATES

Templates are used for cutting out multiple pattern pieces. Made from metal, plastic or card, they may be bought readymade from needlecraft suppliers, or cut out carefully from graph paper glued to strong card or acetate. There are three types (arrows show fabric grain direction, see p. 12):

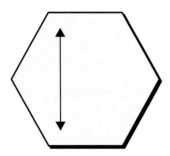 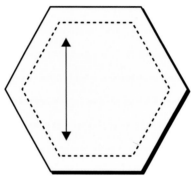

1 Exact size and shape of finished patch, use to cut papers for hand sewing (p. 94). No seam allowance, so cut fabric with 6 mm [¼ in] extra all round.

2 Combines the shape and a 6mm [¼ in] seam allowance. Use when cutting fabric for machine sewing.

3 Inner margin marks actual patch size; outer margin adds seam allowance. Window helps to frame design.

GRAPH PAPER

Graph paper, squared and isometric, will serve both for drafting your overall pattern and drawing individual patches to the precise shape and size you want. Decide which type of template you need (see left).

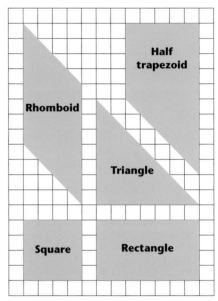

Half trapezoid

Rhomboid

Triangle

Square

Rectangle

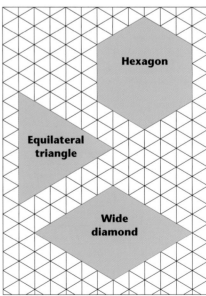

Hexagon

Equilateral triangle

Wide diamond

MAKING TEMPLATES

Cut shapes from the graph paper with care because these will form your templates. Any inaccuracy now becomes a bigger problem at the sewing stage.

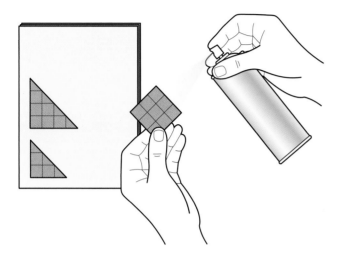

1 With spray adhesive, glue each shape to a sheet of mounting board or acetate.

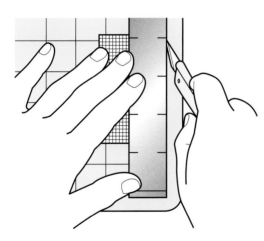

2 Cut out the templates with a sharp craft knife and metal straight edge. Keep fingers clear of the blade.

Mark the templates with an arrow for grain direction and write 'This way up' if there is risk of confusion. Also note how many of each shape you need, and from which fabric.

STANDARD TEMPLATE SHAPES

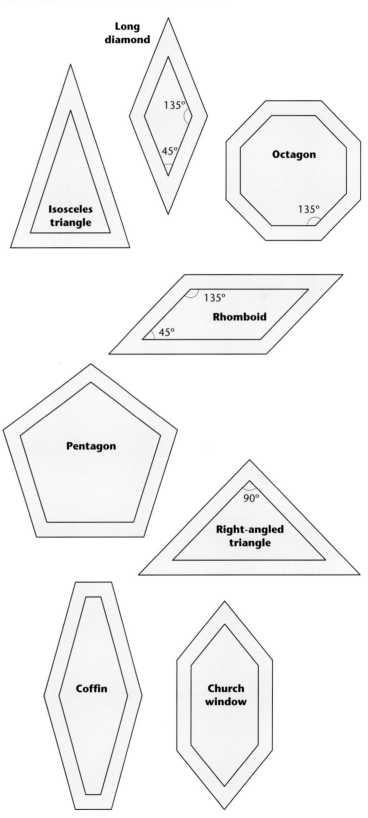

PILLOWCASE WITH ENGLISH PATCHWORK ROSETTE
LEVEL **BEGINNER**

Single-shape hexagon patchwork is traditionally associated with nineteenth-century English hand-sewn designs, made from cotton fabric folded neatly over backing papers.

See template p. 122 and trace or photocopy. The inner hexagon gives the finished patch size and is also a template for the papers. Use the outer margin of the window template for cutting out the patch plus seam allowance.

See pages 92–93 for a fuller explanation of patchwork templates and how to use them.

Take care to cut your papers accurately from the template. You will need seven for each rosette.

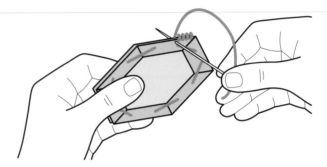

2 Join patches right sides (RS) together and oversew along one side neatly from corner to corner. Practise just catching the fold of fabric each time so that as little as possible shows on the RS.

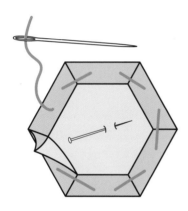

1 Pin the paper to the fabric. Folding the fabric over as you go, tack [baste] through fabric and paper, right around the patch. This holds everything in place until final stitching is done. Prepare all your hexagons this way.

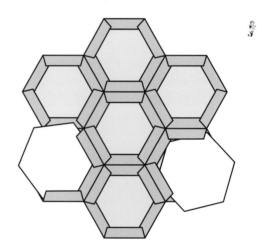

3 Construct a single rosette by first joining six hexagons round a central one. Do not break off your thread but go as far as you can with one length. Tacking stitches and papers stay in place until the final stages of a project.

4 When the rosette is complete, remove tacking and papers. Press face down so the seam allowance doesn't make a ridge on the surface.

5 Pin and tack the patchwork to the pillowcase. Attach it permanently by slip stitching firmly right round the rosette. Press once again.

YOU WILL NEED

- A plain cotton pillowcase
- Scraps of fabric, recycled or new, ready washed and pressed
- An old magazine for cutting patchwork papers
- Tacking [basting] cotton
- Matching thread

The patches on this pillow case are cut from the same fabric used for the quilt and curtains in a child's room. It is quite easy to produce co-ordinated bed-linen in this way.

Truly traditional English patchwork is made from flowery chintz but of course you can work with any pattern fabric you choose. If taking from several sources, try to put together fabrics of the same fibre and weight because the finished piece will look better.

After mastering your first rosette, here are some other combinations of hexagons that you might like to try across other projects, such as placemats, bags, cushions or even a quilt.

Here are two hand-sewing stitches used in patchwork.

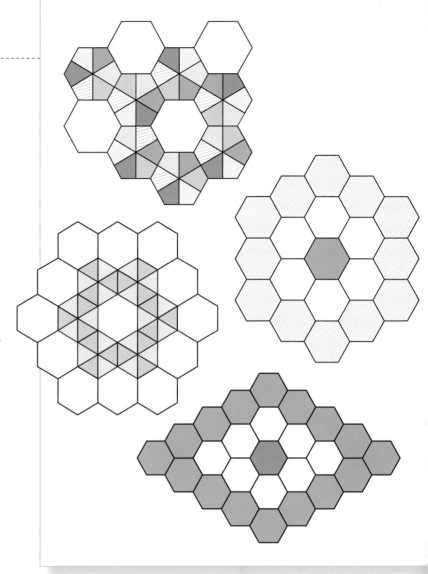

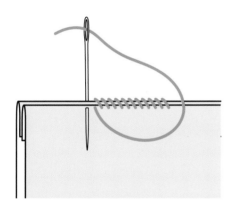

Oversewing or whip stitch Secure thread with two small stitches on the spot and proceed with neat diagonal stitches equally spaced. Sew from left to right or vice versa.

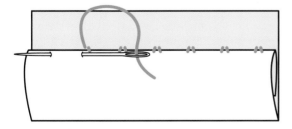

Slip stitch attaches a folded edge invisibly to a flat surface. Take up a few threads of flat fabric with your needle, enter fold and slide along inside before emerging to make the next stitch.

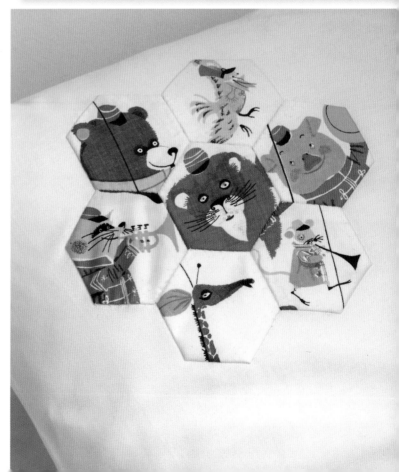

TABLECLOTH WITH PATCHWORK CORNERS
LEVEL INTERMEDIATE

Worked with only two basic shapes, this project introduces the technique of strip-piecing. It would not be difficult to design a scheme that complements your own tableware or décor.

1 Prepare sheeting by cutting and machine hemming to size. Ensure the grain runs straight (p. 12) so that the tablecloth hangs square.

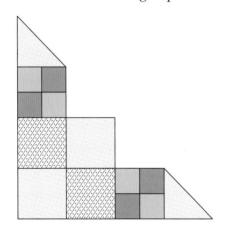

2 Except for the triangles, this patchwork does not use backing papers. Each corner motif consists of four large squares, joined to two more squares that are subdivided into four smaller ones, and finished – Art Deco style – with a pair of triangular 'wing tips'. The blocks are constructed from strips of fabric sewn together, cut across, turned around and re-joined. The main block matches the place mats on pp. 98-99.

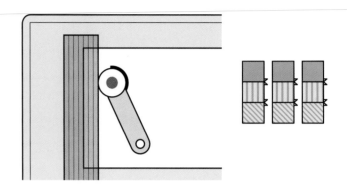

3 Strip-piecing is best done with a rotary cutter, using a dressmaker's ruler and cutting mat for safety. Strips are first sewn vertically, then cut horizontally.

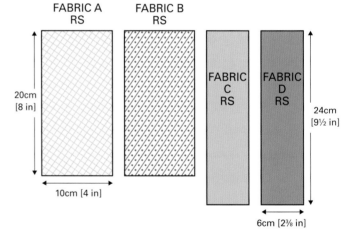

FABRIC A
RS

FABRIC B
RS

FABRIC C
RS

FABRIC D
RS

20cm [8 in]

24cm [9½ in]

10cm [4 in]

6cm [2⅜ in]

YOU WILL NEED

- A plain white tablecloth, or brand new cotton sheeting, pre-shrunk, lightly starched and ironed
- Patchwork fabric, pre-shrunk, starched and ironed
- Matching thread
- Tacking [basting] cotton
- Rotary cutter and ruler OR Dressmaker's shears
- Cutting mat
- Squared maths [math] or graph paper

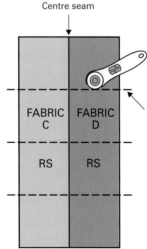

Centre seam

FABRIC C

FABRIC D

RS

RS

4 The strips required for one corner motif involve four different fabrics, A-D. Calculate all seam allowances carefully before cutting your fabric; we allowed 1 cm [⅜ in] for each turning.

5 Once the rectangles have been cut, they are paired up and machined together vertically. Fabrics A/B are then halved horizontally. However, fabrics C/D are divided equally into four (see left).

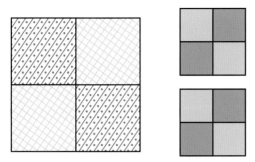

6 Reverse one of the A/B strips from top to bottom and, right sides (RS) facing, tack [baste] and machine both halves together to produce one large square, chequerboard style. Remove tacking [basting] and press seams open.

7 With the large square WS up, fold and iron a 1 cm [⅜ in] turning on all four sides.

8 Both pairs of C/D strips are also machined together chequerboard style (Step 6), producing two new squares. Repeat Step 7.

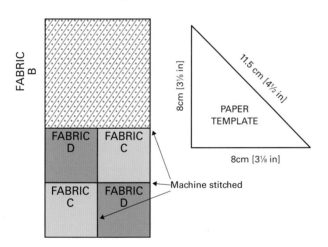

FABRIC B

8cm [3⅛ in]

11.5 cm [4½ in]

PAPER TEMPLATE

8cm [3⅛ in]

FABRIC D | FABRIC C

FABRIC C | FABRIC D

Machine stitched

9 RS together, pin, tack and machine one side of each of the new squares to one side of the main block (Fig 1). Remove tacking and press seams open.

10 The Art Deco 'wing tips' are two right-angled triangles (p.93), which should be formed around full-size templates drawn onto squared or graph paper for accuracy. Pin the paper to WS fabric and cut out with a 1 cm [⅜ in] seam allowance.

11 Tack [baste] the fabric triangles around the papers (p. 94). Tuck under or trim back excess fabric from the pointed ends. Apply a little fray stopper WS if necessary. RS facing, oversew triangles neatly (p. 95) to either end. Leave tacking in place. Iron carefully both sides.

12 Working on a flat surface, pin the patchwork on the corner of the tablecloth. Tack securely around the motif, smoothing out the fabric as you go. Machine stitch the motif to the sheeting with a 5 mm [⅛ in] margin. Go right to the tips of the triangles. Change direction by stopping with the needle down, raising the foot and pulling the fabric gently around; lower the foot before starting to stitch again. Finally, remove all tacking and iron. Spray starch for a smooth finish.

FOUR PLACE MATS
LEVEL INTERMEDIATE

Each finished place mat measures 33 cm [13 in] square. Your fabrics can be new or recycled but they should be pre-shrunk and of similar weight.

Prepare eight 19 cm [7½ in] squares from each cover design to give sixteen squares in total. Divide backing fabric into four 38 x 38 cm [15 x 15 in] pieces. The seam allowance is 12 mm [½ in].

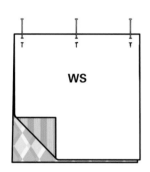

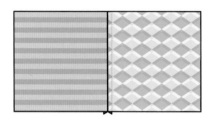

1 To make one mat: right sides (RS) facing, pin and stitch together one square of each cover design with 12 mm [½ in] seam allowance, to produce two pairs of squares.

FOR FOUR MATS YOU WILL NEED

- Two pieces of fabric 76 x 38 cm [30 x 15 in] in two different designs for the top cover
- One piece 76 x 76 cm [30 x 30 in] for backing
- Four pieces thin wadding [batting] 35.5 x 35.5 cm [14 x 14 in] for interlining
- Matching threads

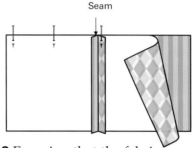

2 Ensuring that the fabric squares fall in a chequerboard formation, RS facing, pin and stitch the two strips together. Press seams open.

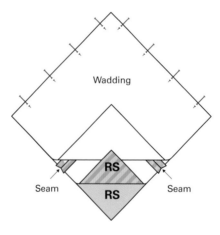

3 Lay backing and patchwork RS together. Place the square of wadding [batting] on top of both. Pin and stitch through all three layers on all four sides, leaving an opening of 15 cm [6 in] on one side. Snip corners and turn RS out. Close the opening by hand stitching. Top stitch around the perimeter.

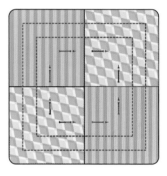

4 If you wish to quilt the placemat, machine stitch a line 2.5 cm [1 in] in from the edge, marking this with pins or using a quilting foot as a guide.

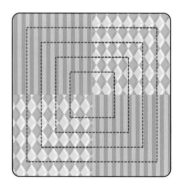

5 For further quilting, mark parallel lines in from the previous ones and finish by stitching around the perimeter.

Repeat to make a set of
four placemats.

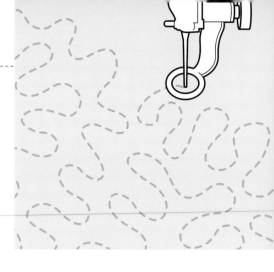

FILLING PATTERNS

Filling patterns are used to quilt background spaces around individual motifs, or they may be used on their own to quilt an entire project. These overall patterns are an excellent treatment for larger areas, not only for the decorative effect but also to ensure that the wadding [batting] layer of a quilt doesn't bunch up. On a smaller scale, they look good on thinly padded panels for cushion covers and box lids.

Straight-line patterns are the quickest. If you have one, attach a spacer foot that enables you to stitch parallel lines automatically. Otherwise, use an acrylic ruler and fabric pen to mark out lines at regular intervals. For a wavy filler pattern, try using a circular or oval plate. Place it on your quilt top and draw along one edge, reversing the edge as you go along.

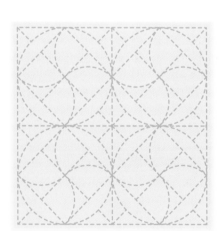 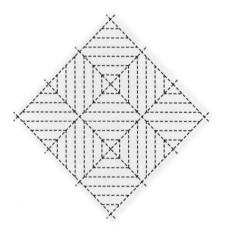

FREE MOTION QUILTING

Free motion quilting (also called 'free machine') is performed with a darning or embroidery foot and the feed dogs lowered or covered with a special plate (p. 10). The sewing machine manual will show you how to operate the drop feed mechanism, usually via a simple lever. A wooden embroidery hoop can also be used for smaller areas; in this case the rim is turned uppermost so that the wrong side of the fabric is flat against the needle plate.

Free motion doesn't need marking out first. Because the tiny metal teeth of the feed dogs aren't engaged and you have set your stitch length to zero, you are free to move the quilting in any direction. You will need to practice coordinating the stitch speed and movement of the fabric. It's important to run the machine at a constant speed in order to maintain a consistent stitch length. The general rule is to stitch fast but move the fabric slowly. Use a thread slightly darker than the colour of the top layer if you want the quilting to blend in.

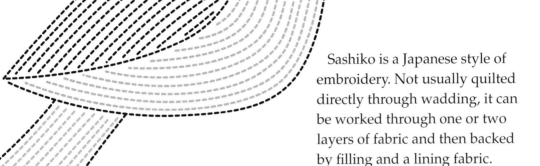

KANTHA AND SASHIKO

Try creating other filling patterns with these traditional hand-stitching techniques, using cotton embroidery threads like perle [pearl] twist or stranded cotton [floss], plus a long needle with a large eye, such as a large 'sharp' or crewel needle. Kantha is a decorative technique from Bangladesh. Sewn predominantly with a running stitch in different coloured threads, it is worked through several layers of fine cotton fabric or lawn without wadding [batting], although you could use a very thin filling material.

Kantha uses both stylized motifs and pictorial design. One colour is used to stitch the outline of a motif, like the bird shown here. The inside is filled with regular rows in various complementary colours. The background is stitched with a thread matching the background fabric.

Sashiko is a Japanese style of embroidery. Not usually quilted directly through wadding, it can be worked through one or two layers of fabric and then backed by filling and a lining fabric.

Long ago, Japanese working men wore indigo-dyed jackets made from two layers of hemp or cotton fabric and the women stitched these layers together for durability. They traditionally used white thread on a dark blue background and sashiko needles 5 cm [2 in] long with a uniform shaft. The stitch pattern for everyday wear was fairly plain but evolved into elaborate designs for special occasions.

CLASSIC FRAME QUILT
LEVEL INTERMEDIATE/ADVANCED

The 'frame' quilt was a clever device of early quiltmakers for creating an eye-catching quilt when they had only a small but special piece of fabric and plenty of something else more ordinary. They would place the interesting piece at the centre and then use strips of complementary fabrics to 'frame' it. This was also a very quick and simple way to make a quilt.

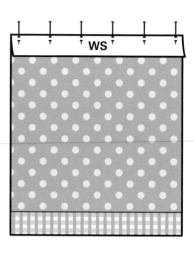

It is not necessary to use a novelty fabric. You could have quite an ordinary centre panel but still produce a remarkable quilt, especially if you are working towards a particular colour scheme.

The finished quilt is approximately 100 cm [40 in] square. To make it larger, you need to add extra strips to the frame and enlarge the backing and wadding [batting] accordingly. It can be sewn by hand or machine

If you want a lightweight quilt for use in hot weather, you could recycle an old sheet as the filling, instead of wadding.

Use 100 per cent cotton fabric and thread for a classic result. Fabrics involved can be new or recycled but should be pre-shrunk and of a similar weight.

All strips include a 15 mm [½ in] seam allowance. This quilt top features three different-patterned fabrics, which we have labelled A, B and C. A fourth one (D) – of equivalent texture and weight – serves as the quilt backing.

Using a cutting mat, acrylic ruler and rotary cutter, from Fabric A cut out the central panel 63.5 cm [25 in] square.

1 Cut two strips of Fabric B, 12.5 x 63.5 cm [5 x 25 in]. Right sides (RS) together, pin along two opposite sides of the central panel. Stitch both strips to the panel. Press seams outwards towards the open edges.

2 Measure and cut two more strips of Fabric B, 12.5 x 84 cm [5 x 33 in]. As before, RS facing, pin then stitch the strips along the remaining two sides of the central panel. Press seams outwards towards the open edges.

YOU WILL NEED

- Fabric A One 63.5 cm [25 in] square, which forms the centre panel
- Fabric B 93.5 x 57.5 cm [36¾ x 22⅝ in]
- Fabric C 113 x 57.5 cm [44½ x 22⅝ in]
- Fabric D (backing) 113 cm [44½ in] square
- Wadding [batting] 113 cm [44½ in] square (final size)
- Matching threads
- Embroidery silk [floss] for tying (optional)

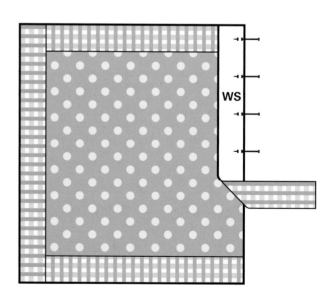

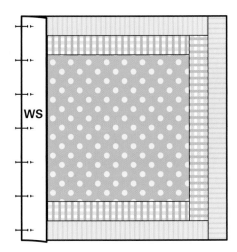

3 Take Fabric C, cut two strips 12.5 x 84 cm [5 x 33 in] and two more 12.5 x 104 cm [5 x 41 in]. Attach them in opposite pairs, as for the central panel. Press seams outwards and then press the entire quilt top.

4 Measure and cut a piece 113 cm [44½ in] square of the wadding and also of the backing, Fabric D. Smooth out the wadding and lay the quilt top RS up on top of it. The top will be slightly smaller all round than the wadding. Place the square of backing RS down over the quilt top.

Pin the three layers together all around the perimeter, smoothing them as you go, carefully aligning the edges of the quilt top with the backing. Stitch around the perimeter of the backing fabric with 12 mm [½ in] seam allowance but leave an opening of about 30 cm [12 in]. Ensure you are sewing right through the quilt back, top and wadding.

Use your rotary cutter, mat and ruler to trim any bits of wadding that protrude beyond

the quilt top. Snip the four corners and turn it all RS out. Smooth all three layers outwards from the centre. Close the 30 cm [12 in] opening by hand with small neat stitches.

Lining fabric
WS

RS

RS

Quilt top

Wadding

Quilting Try traditional tufting [tying] at intervals of 15 cm [6 in] along the seam lines and also on the central panel. Mark the quilt top at regular intervals with long pins, then thread up with 6 strands of embroidery silk [floss]. Single back-stitch (p 14) around each pin and cut the thread, leaving 4 cm [1½ in] free ends to tie in a double knot. Trim ends to about 20 mm [¾ in] above the surface.

BEAN BAGS
LEVEL BEGINNER

Tetra-shaped bean bags for soft play or juggling can be any size. These measure 12 cm [4¾ in] along the edges and the fabric was constructed from String Patchwork using a rotary cutter (p. 96). Machine stitch for strong seams.

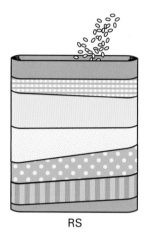

1 Wash and iron fabrics and trim fraying threads. Cut into strips roughly 2.5 x 12.5 cm [1 x 5½ in]. It doesn't matter if they vary and the sides aren't parallel.

2 Right sides (RS) together, machine stitch each strip to the next one with a 7 mm (¼ in) seam allowance, until you have a piece of fabric the size you want.

3 On WS, press all seam allowances in one direction. Trim string patchwork to a rectangle twice as long as its width.

4 Fold in half, RS together and, with a 12 mm [½ in] seam allowance, stitch up sides to form a small bag. Snip corners and turn RS out.

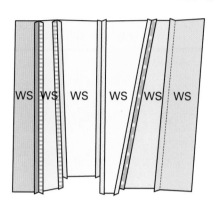

WS WS WS WS WS WS

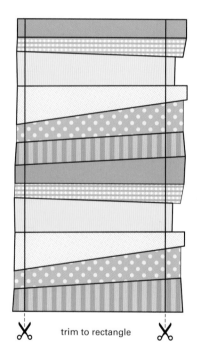

trim to rectangle

YOU WILL NEED

- Long thin scraps and left-overs of cotton [calico] material in as many colours and patterns as you can find
- (These bags may also be made from any single piece of fabric. Cut a strip twice as long as your chosen width and follow the instructions from Step 4)
- Neutral-coloured thread
- Uncooked popcorn, rice, split peas or plastic pellets for filling

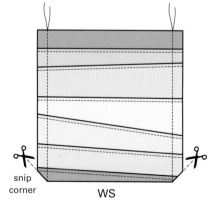

snip corner   WS

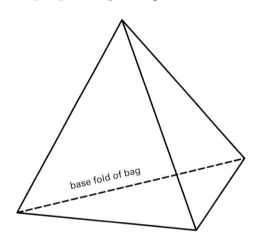

RS

5 Three-quarters fill the bag with uncooked popcorn, rice, split peas or plastic pellets.

base fold of bag

6 Turn the raw edges of the bag in at the top and, holding it at halfway points X and Y, pull the mouth tight to form a straight line at right-angles to the bottom fold. Tack [baste] the bag closed.

7 Finally, top stitch by machine between points X and Y. Sew in the loose ends. Remove tacking.

PATCHWORK BALL
LEVEL BEGINNER

This soft felt ball can be stitched either by hand or machine.

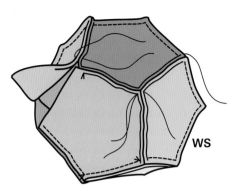

WS

1 Trace or copy a pentagon (p. 93) and make an accurate template from paper or card.

2 The ball depends on the perfect fit of every piece. Carefully cut twelve patches from your felt, by pinning on the paper pattern or drawing round the card with fabric marker.

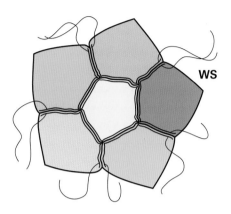

WS

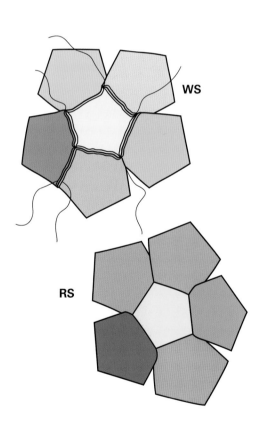

WS

RS

3 Assemble two rosettes of six patches with a seam allowance of 3 mm [⅛ in]. Make the centres two different colours to avoid same-colour patches ending up adjacent at the final stage.

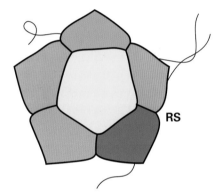

RS

4 Working wrong side (WS) out, join the sides of the patches to form two bowl shapes. Turn right sides (RS) out and decide how you will join them into a ball without sewing the same colours together.

5 Working on WS again, join the halves with 3 mm seam allowance. Leave 5 mm [³⁄₁₆ in] unsewn at either end of every patch, together with thread long enough to stitch up each trio of corners before filling. Two sides of the final patch must be left open for this purpose.

6 Thread up a fine needle and begin closing each set of three corners. Stitch neatly and firmly because the filling will put pressure on these points. You can fasten off with knots – no one will see this side of your work again!

7 Turn RS out and stuff as firmly as possible with polyester filling. Close the remaining two sides with ladder or slip stitch (p. 15).

YOU WILL NEED

- Scraps of felt in at least six different colours
- A pentagon template
- Neutral-coloured thread
- Synthetic filler

MULE SLIPPERS
LEVEL INTERMEDIATE/ADVANCED

These slippers can be made in any material from silk to leather, provided you use the correct needles. Thick, soft fabrics work well, such as blanket, fleece, cotton waffle and terry towelling.

1 Using a photocopier, enlarge the shapes on pp. 122–123 and cut out the materials as instructed on the pattern pieces.

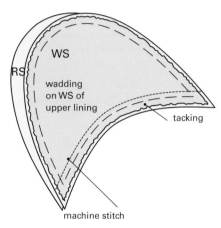

2 Tack [baste] the 2 oz wadding [batting] to the wrong side (WS) of the lining half of each upper section.

3 With the two halves of the uppers right sides (RS) together, machine around the inner curve with 12 mm [½ in] seam allowance.

4 Clip curves, layer the seam allowances if too bulky, turn to RS and press. Trim the excess fabric 'ears' from the pointed ends of the uppers and tack around the toe to hold the layers in line. Attach the ribbon trim over the instep, if desired.

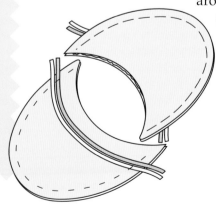

YOU WILL NEED

- Half a metre [yard] of main fabric
- Approximately 35 cm [13¾ in] square piece of anti-skid sole fabric (Jiffy Grip or Slipper Gripper)
- Approximately 35 cm [13¾ in] square piece of 6 oz wadding [batting] for inner soles
- Approximately 40 x 20 cm [16 x 8 in] 2 oz wadding [batting] for uppers
- 1.5 metres [yards] bias binding 2.5 cm [1 in] wide
- 46 cm [18 in] ribbon trim (optional)
- Matching threads

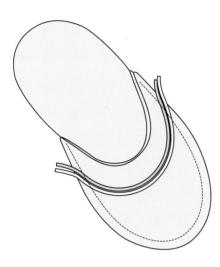

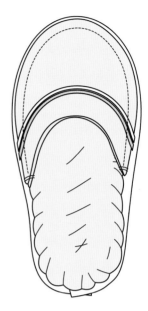

7 Holding the slipper upside down, tack the sole wadding in position with just two or three large Xs, they will be removed later on.

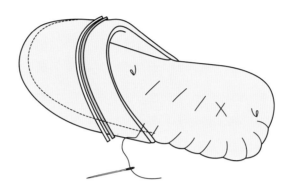

5 Tack the uppers onto the inner soles of each slipper, matching the the three star points indicated on the sole template. Make sure the pair mirror each other perfectly and then machine stitch the uppers in place with 12 mm [½ in] seam allowance

8 Oversew the inner sole to enclose the wadding. The stitches should not be pulled so tight that they compress or distort the wadding.

10 Set the padded slippers into the prepared gripper soles and pin all round before tacking. Pay special attention to the star points where the uppers arch over the instep.

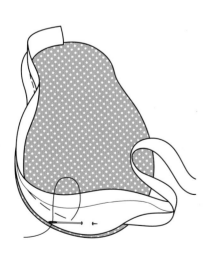

9 With similar large stitches, continue tacking around the sole, and attach the wadding to the underside of the upper section. It is important to use only the inner layer of the seam allowance at this point. You will not be removing this stitching, so choose a pale colour thread.

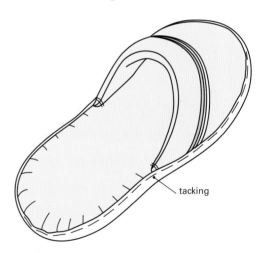

tacking

11 Slip stitch the remaining (folded) edge of the bias binding right around the slipper for a neat finish.

12 Remove all visible tacking thread.

6 RS together, tack and stitch one side of the bias binding around the perimeter of each gripper sole and turn RS out.

TABLET CASE
LEVEL INTERMEDIATE

1 Cut out two pieces of cover fabric 43 x 28 cm [17 x 11 in]. Round off the eight corners by using a compass or tracing around a 2.5 cm [1 in] coin. Cut one piece in half on the long side to produce two new sections for the inner cover, measuring 28 x 21.7 cm [11 x 8½ in].

Fastening tab
Cut two

Grain

← 4 cm →
[1½ in]

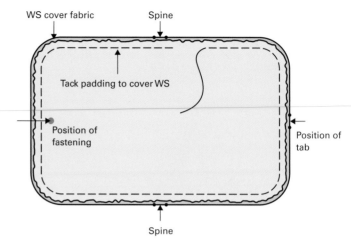

WS cover fabric   Spine

Tack padding to cover WS

Position of fastening

Position of tab

Spine

2 Copy or trace the tab shape and cut three; one layer interfaces between the outer pair. The large dot indicates the centre of the closure and should be marked on the right side (RS) of one of the outer pieces. Attach one half of your chosen closure directly over the dot. With wrong sides (WS) together, tack [baste] all three layers around the edge, leaving the straight end open.

4 Attach padding to WS of outer cover. Left to right, flip the cover to RS. Fix the other half of the closure to the spot indicated, 2.5 cm [1 in] in from the raw edge. Tack the fastening tab in place halfway down the opposite (left-hand) side, raw edges matching, so the tip of the tab points inwards and the closure lies face up.

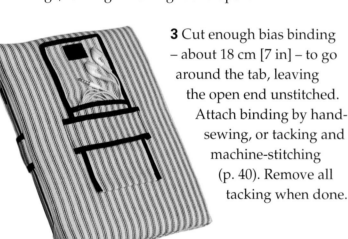

3 Cut enough bias binding – about 18 cm [7 in] – to go around the tab, leaving the open end unstitched. Attach binding by hand-sewing, or tacking and machine-stitching (p. 40). Remove all tacking when done.

5 Cut a strip of fabric 12 cm [4¾ in] long and the same 4 cm [1½ in] width as the fastening tab. This will be the strap that holds the wallet for the earpieces. Bias bind the two long edges and tack the raw ends under 7 mm [¼ in] at either end. Press the turnings neatly, which will make it easier to top stitch the strap into position. It should be in line with the tab and 5 cm [2 in] from the point where the tab joins the cover.

YOU WILL NEED

- 60 x 60 cm [24 x 24 in] cover fabric such as twill, canvas, denim, or furnishing fabric
- 40 x 26 cm [15½ x 10 in] wadding [batting], fleece or thick felt for interfacing
- 1.5 metres [yards] bias binding
- 80 cm [32 in] flat tape or grosgrain ribbon 19 mm [¾ in] wide
- Small magnetic clasp, large snap fastener or Velcro for closure
- Two pieces of cardboard each 25 x 19 cm [9¾ x 7½ in]
- Matching threads

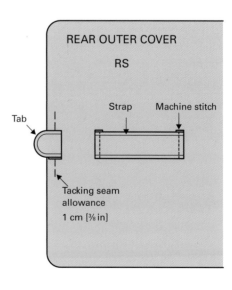

REAR OUTER COVER

RS

Tab   Strap   Machine stitch

Tacking seam allowance 1 cm [⅜ in]

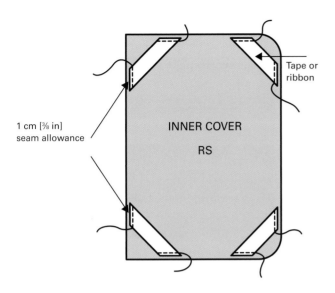

1 cm [⅜ in] seam allowance

INNER COVER

RS

Tape or ribbon

6 Cut four 10 cm [4 in] lengths of the straight tape or grosgrain ribbon. Tack and stitch one length to each corner of the right-hand inner cover half, as shown.

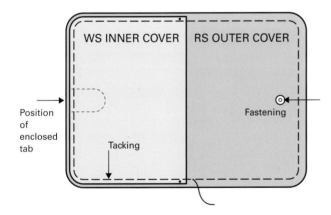

WS INNER COVER   RS OUTER COVER

Position of enclosed tab

Tacking

Fastening

7 RS facing, pin and tack the ribboned inner half to the outer cover with the tab pointing inwards.

8 RS facing, pin and tack the remaining inner half to the other half of the outer cover. Machine stitch around the perimeter of the case, joining the inner and outer covers with a seam allowance of 1 cm [⅜ in].

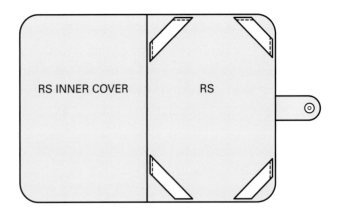

RS INNER COVER   RS

9 Turn both halves of the cover RS out and remove all tacking.

10 Round off the two outer corners of each piece of cardboard (see Step 1) and slide one into each of the openings inside the cover. Tack down both openings to hold the card in place.

11 Take the remaining straight tape or grosgrain ribbon and trim to fit the height of the case plus a 1 cm [⅜ in] turning at either end. Tack, then hem stitch both sides in place, enclosing ribbon ends and the raw edges of the cover openings. Remove tacking.

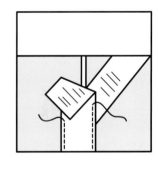

12 Cut a strip of cover fabric 29.5 x 8 cm [11⅝ x 3⅛ in] to make the detachable wallet for your earpieces (see p. 123). Bias bind the lower edge first (p. 40). The wallet fabric is folded twice, as shown, so that the lower edge comes up to form the opening. Starting at the lower fold, tack then stitch binding around the rest of the wallet. This joins the sides of the wallet together and also encloses the raw edges of the overlapping flap. Use small snap fasteners or Velcro to fasten the flap to the lower section, once it has been slotted through the strap on the cover.

CLUTCH BAG
LEVEL BEGINNER/INTERMEDIATE

A soft, unstructured clutch bag with a rouleau wrist loop, designed to be made quickly and easily, and doubly attractive when it matches a dress made for a special occasion. Seam allowance is 1 cm [½ in] unless otherwise stated. Work only in metric or imperial measurements, do not mix the two.

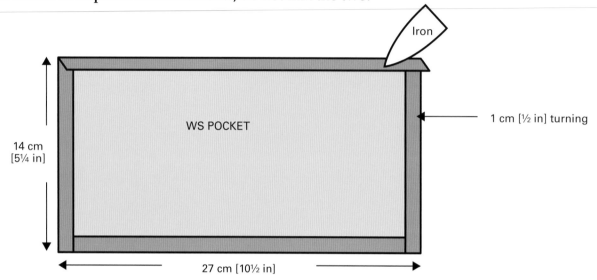

Iron

WS POCKET

14 cm [5¼ in]

1 cm [½ in] turning

27 cm [10½ in]

1 Cut rectangles measuring 49 x 29 cm [19½ x 11½ in] from both dress and lining fabrics.

2 From remaining dress fabric, cut a continuous bias strip, 30 x 2.5 cm (12 x 1 in), for the wrist loop. If you have insufficient fabric on the bias, cut on the grain instead (p. 12).

3 From remaining lining fabric, cut a rectangle 16 x 29 cm [6¼ x 11½ in] for the inside pocket. Final size, 14 x 13.5 cm [5¼ x 5¼ in].

4 With pocket fabric wrong side (WS) up, iron a 1 cm [½ in] turning on all four sides (see above).

YOU WILL NEED

- 0.5 metre [½ yard] or one 'fat quarter' [18 x 22 in] of dress fabric
- The same quantity of lining fabric
- 49 x 29 cm [19½ x 11½ in] interlining such as heavy Vilene, craft felt or very thin wadding [batting]
- Lightweight magnetic bag clasp, 12 mm [½ in]
- Large silk flower
- Matching threads
- Loop turner for rouleau
- Seam ripper or craft knife
- Cutting mat or thick card

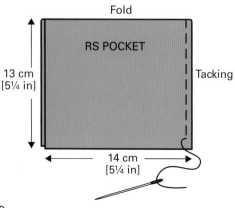

Fold

RS POCKET

13 cm [5¼ in]

Tacking

14 cm [5¼ in]

5 WS together, fold and iron pocket fabric in half. Join halves by tacking [basting] around the open sides for a self-lined pocket front with no raw edges.

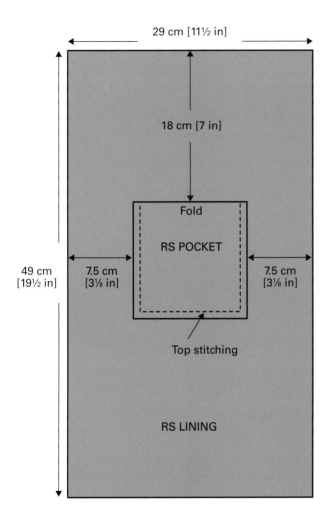

29 cm [11½ in]

18 cm [7 in]

Fold

RS POCKET

49 cm [19½ in]

7.5 cm [3⅛ in]

7.5 cm [3⅛ in]

Top stitching

RS LINING

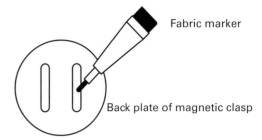

Fabric marker

Back plate of magnetic clasp

9 Turn lining to WS and make a dot with a fabric marker 4.5 cm [1¾ in] from the top edge and 14.5 cm [5¾ in] from either side. Take the back plate of the magnetic clasp, centre it on the dot and draw a line through each slot as a cutting guide.

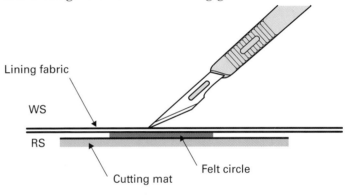

Lining fabric

WS

RS

Felt circle

Cutting mat

10 With one felt circle centred under the dot and sandwiched between cutting mat and RS of fabric, follow the markings and cut two short slits through WS of fabric and the felt. Use a seam ripper or sharp craft knife. Take great care to keep fingers clear.

6 Lay lining flat, right side (RS) up. With folded edge at the top, pin pocket front 18 cm [7 in] from top edge of lining, with 7.5 cm [3⅛ in] either side.

7 Tack, then top-stitch pocket front to lining with 4 mm [⅛ in]] seam allowance. Remove tacking and press.

8 Cut two 4 cm [1½ in] circles of scrap felt or thin wadding for reinforcement behind the magnetic clasp.

11 On WS, match cuts in felt circle with slots in back plate and hold together while pushing the prongs of the clasp through from RS. Lay the assembly on a firm surface and press prongs inwards on either side.

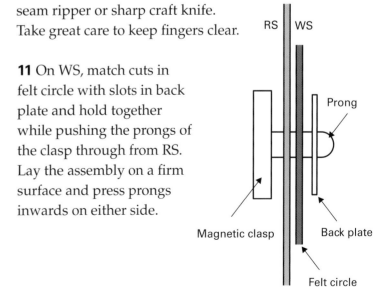

Fabric

RS | WS

Prong

Magnetic clasp

Back plate

Felt circle

12 To attach the other half of the clasp, turn to WS of dress fabric piece and make a dot with the fabric marker 11 cm [4¼ in] from the lower edge and 14.5 cm [5¾ in] from either side. From that point, repeat Steps 9-11.

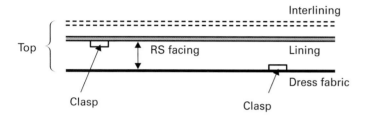

13 Assemble all three layers of the bag as shown above. Pin, tack and machine stitch them together with 1 cm [½ in] seam allowance. On one long side, leave a 9 cm [3½ in] opening.

14 Clip corners and turn bag RS out through opening. Push corners out firmly before slip-stitching the opening closed. Press with a cloth on the lining side if necessary but treat delicate fabrics with care, it may be best to leave them unpressed.

15 Construct the rouleau wrist loop as shown on p. 59. Sew with 5mm [³⁄₁₆ in] seam allowance. Apply fray stopper to raw ends if necessary.

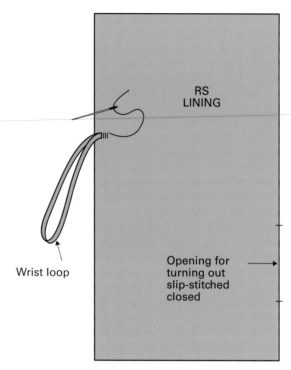

16 Bend rouleau in half and, both ends together, hand-stitch about 1cm [½ in] to the left side of the lining, 28.5 cm [11¼ in] up from the lower edge.

17 Fold up the lower 15.5 cm [6 in] of the bag. Pin and tack up both sides, taking in the ends of the wrist loop. Top-stitch the sides by machine with a seam allowance of 1 cm [⅜ in]. Alternatively, ladder stitch (p. 15) the edges of the lining firmly together by hand, so there is no external stitching to be seen.

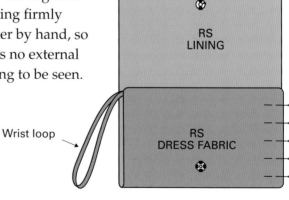

18 As a finishing touch, sew a large silk flower to the top of the flap.

SQUARE-BASED TOTE BAG
LEVEL **INTERMEDIATE/ADVANCED**

A heavy duty tote bag, built for shopping or carrying college books. The best fabrics to use would be canvas, twill or denim, with a close-woven cotton lining.

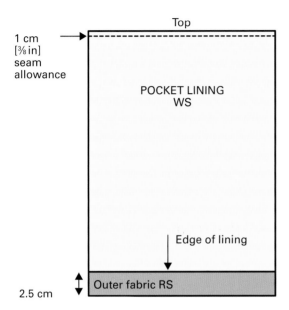

1 Pin the pocket fabric and lining right sides (RS) together and stitch at the top end with 1 cm [⅜ in] seam allowance.

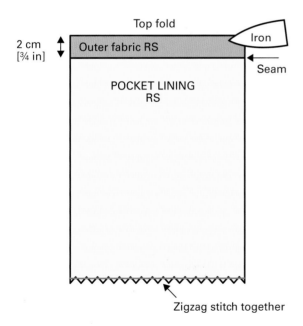

2 Flip to RS and pull the lower edges level, forcing outer fabric to fold over at the top. Sew and enclose the raw edges together with zigzag stitch. Press the top fold.

3 Fold the lower edge of the pocket 3 cm [1³⁄₁₆ in] upwards and inwards, and press. Fold the main bag fabric in half but do not press.

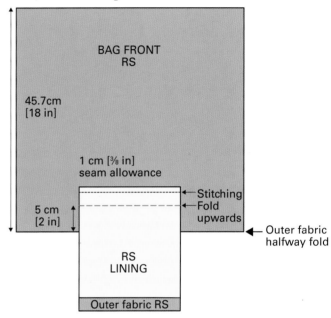

4 Centre the pocket on the bag width and position the base fold 5 cm [2 in] from the fold of the bag. Open out the pocket, then pin, tack [baste] and stitch the end to the bag front with 1 cm [⅜ in] seam allowance.

YOU WILL NEED

- Outer fabric 91.5 x 56 cm [36 x 22 in] (includes 2.5 cm [1 in] seam allowance)
- Lining fabric 91.5 x 56 cm [36 x 22 in] (includes 2.5 cm [1 in] seam allowance)
- Pocket fabric 28 x 21 cm [11 x 8¼ in]
- Pocket lining fabric 25.5 x 21 cm [10 x 8¼ in]
- 5 metres [5½ yards] jute webbing, 5 cm [2 in] wide
- Matching threads
- 42 x 9.5 cm [16½ x 3¾ in] base stiffener of plastic canvas or thick cardboard
- 4 Bag feet
- Fabric marker
- Seam ripper or craft knife

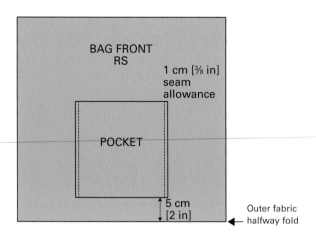

BAG FRONT
RS

1 cm [⅜ in]
seam
allowance

POCKET

5 cm
[2 in]

Outer fabric
halfway fold

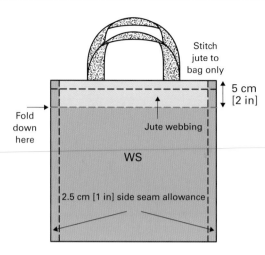

Stitch
jute to
bag only

5 cm
[2 in]

Fold
down
here

Jute webbing

WS

2.5 cm [1 in] side seam allowance

Fold

5 Fold the pocket upwards again and stitch each side with 1 cm [⅜ in] seam allowance. Allow slight ease on the pocket width.

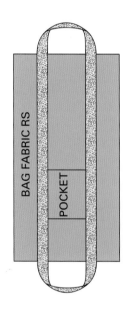

BAG FABRIC RS

POCKET

6 Lay the main bag fabric completely flat, RS up. Turn under and pin 5 cm [2 in] at each end. Measure a continuous length of jute webbing to cover twice the visible length of the bag, not forgetting to include 46 cm [18 in] for each handle and 5 cm [2 in] overlap at the join. The webbing will conceal the raw edges of the pocket fabric, leaving a 17.2 cm [6 ¾ in] wide opening.

8 Turn to the wrong side (WS) and for strength, insert two pieces of webbing inside the top turnings, leave 2.5 cm [1 in] short at each end to reduce bulk when closing the sides. Attach the webbing to each turning with a line of horizontal stitching that will not show on the finished bag. Seam up each side with 2.5 cm [1 in] allowance and finally fold down the top edge.

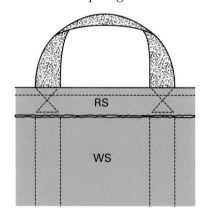

RS

WS

7 Starting at the base of the bag, pin the jute up and down one side. Before sewing begins, unpin the 5 cm [2 in] turnings but do not stitch into them at this stage. Machine along both edges of the webbing. Repeat on the other side, finishing back at the base of the bag. Jute frays readily, secure the cut ends with zigzag stitching.

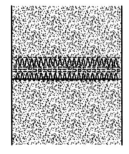

9 Top-stitch an X through all four layers at the base of each handle.

10 Make a crease 18 cm [7 in] long in the middle of each handle and stitch the open edges together.

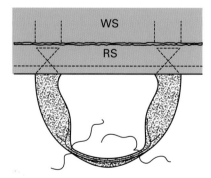

WS

RS

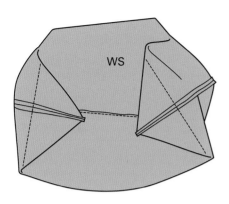

11 To square off the base, align the side seams of the bag with the original base fold (Step 3) to form two triangles with seams down the middle. The base of the triangle dictates the width of the bag, here it is 9.5 cm [3¾ in]. Measure and mark, then stitch along the line. You can either trim off the points of the triangles or press them flat under the base stiffener. Turn the bag to the RS.

12 On the base, mark the webbing where you wish to insert the four bag feet. With great care, cut a slit in the webbing and the bag fabric all the way through, using a seam ripper or craft knife. Push the prongs of the feet up through the slits and fold them outwards like wings. Fit the base stiffener over top.

13 Some bag makers like to enclose the bag stiffener in a tightly fitting cloth sleeve first.

This helps to protect the outer fabric from wearing through against a hard edge or corner.

14 The lining is largely made up the same way as the outer fabric, minus the webbing. Before sewing up the sides, you have the opportunity to add interior pockets of any size or shape that you please. You could also fasten the pockets with Velcro (p. 71), snap fasteners or buttons (p. 58).

15 Slip the lining inside the outer bag and push it well into the corners of the square base. Fold the raw edge down to within 1.5 cm [⅝ in] of the top of the bag and slip stitch neatly all the way round.

XMAS STOCKING
LEVEL BEGINNER

Each square on the grid pattern represents 4 cm [1½ in] but if you alter the value, you can make this stocking to any size you wish. See p. 124.

1 Draw up, scan or copy the stocking shape to the desired size and cut a template from paper.

2 Fold the fabric into four, pin the paper pattern on top and cut out four stocking shapes. Two should show the right side (RS) and two the wrong side (WS) of the material.

3 With the layers as follows: WS up, RS up, WS up, RS up, machine them all together with a seam allowance of 15 mm [½ in], remembering to leave the opening at the top.

4 To finish the raw edges, fold the bias binding in half around the edge of the shape – except for the top – and tack [baste] firmly through all the layers. Machine stitch the binding into place.

5 Cut 38 cm [15 in] of the flat tape to form the hanging loop. Attach to the top back of the stocking with one or two holding stitches.

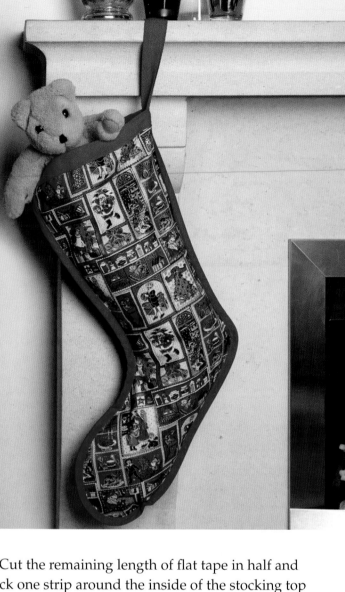

6 Cut the remaining length of flat tape in half and tack one strip around the inside of the stocking top and one around the outside to form a neat band with their raw ends folded under. This bandserves both to secure the hanging loop and conceal the raw edges of the opening.

7 Machine stitch the top band along both sides for a firm finish.

YOU WILL NEED

- 0.5 metre [½ yard] cotton fabric with seasonal pattern, for a self-lined stocking approximately 60 cm [24 in] long from top to toe
- 140 cm [55 in] bias binding trim, 2.5 cm [1 in] wide
- 130 cm [51 in] matching flat tape, 2.5 cm [1 in] wide, for inner and outer top band, and hanging loop
- Matching threads

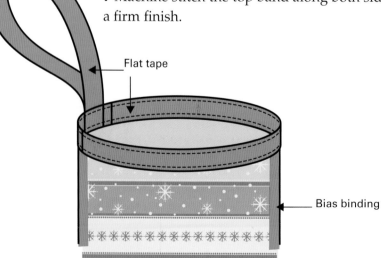

Flat tape

Bias binding

QUICK MAKE: BIRD KEY FOB
LEVEL BEGINNER

All you need is a metal key ring – perhaps recycled from a worn-out fob – and from a few scraps and buttons, you can make a welcome gift in about an hour.

1 This is a same-size template, so you can copy, scan or trace the bird directly from the page. Pin the paper pattern to a piece of felt and cut out two bird bodies. Cut a third bird shape from non-woven interlining or an extra layer of felt.

2 Cut the wing out from the original template. Pin and cut two wing pieces from contrasting felt.

3 Do the same with the tail and crest shapes.

4 Sandwich the interlining between the outer body pieces and hold all three layers together by sewing on two little buttons for eyes, back-to-back either side of the head.

5 Take the length of tape, loop it around the key ring and slide the ends at least 12mm [½in] between the layers at the tail end. Secure with three or four cross stitches on the spot.

6 Thread up with two or three strands of embroidery cotton or plain sewing thread and sew around the bird's body with small, even blanket stitch (p. 15). Use back stitch for a firm attachment when you come to the loop ends caught in the tail, the weight of the keys could put quite a strain on this point.

7 Sew the wings to the body, holding all three layers together by sewing two little buttons on either side, as you did for the eyes.

8 Stick the crest halves to the top of the head and back-to-back to each other by gluing the inner surfaces.

9 Do the same with the tail pieces, which will also neatly cover the stitching around the tail loop and serve to strengthen it at the same time.

YOU WILL NEED

- An empty metal key ring
- A small piece of heavy interlining (Vilene or an extra layer of felt)
- Scraps of coloured felt
- Embroidery cotton [floss]
- Matching sewing thread
- 4 tiny buttons
- Straight tape or ribbon, about 12 mm [½ in wide] and 5 cm [2 in] long
- PVA fabric glue

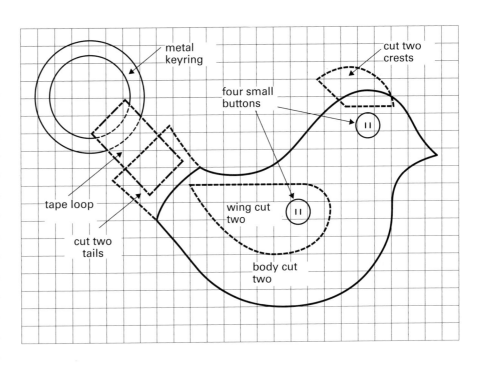

PATTERNS AND TEMPLATES FOR ENLARGEMENT

These patterns are to various scales. Each grid is marked with the square value. Read any additional instructions with care.

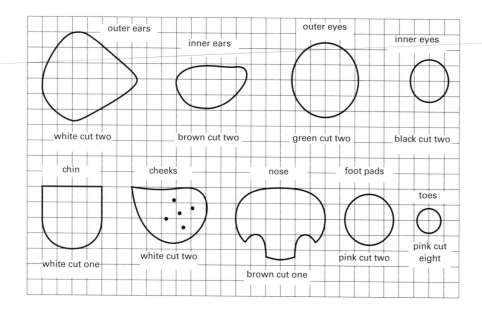

outer ears
inner ears
white cut two
brown cut two

outer eyes
inner eyes
green cut two
black cut two

chin
cheeks
white cut one
white cut two
brown cut one

nose
foot pads
pink cut two

toes
pink cut eight

FELT GLOVE PUPPET
PAGE 16

1 square = 5 mm [³⁄₁₆ in]
Enlarge shapes by 30% via photocopier.

Copy or trace Tiger's features and cut them from different coloured felts. Use the photograph as a guide to the black stripes

APPLIQUED SHOE BAG
PAGE 30

1 square = 5 mm [³⁄₁₆ in]
Enlarge shapes by 150%

outline for shoe upper and outer sole

upper cut from purple felt outer sole cut from white

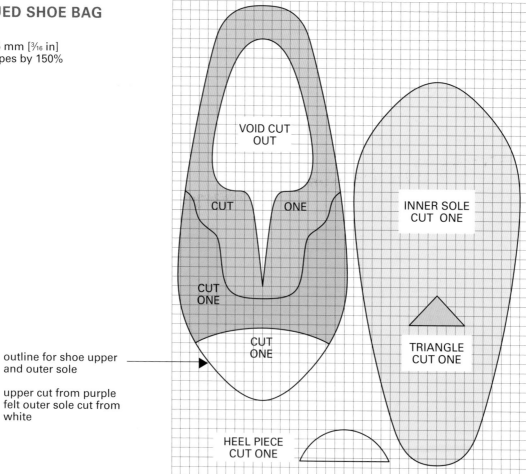

VOID CUT OUT

CUT ONE

CUT ONE

CUT ONE

INNER SOLE CUT ONE

TRIANGLE CUT ONE

HEEL PIECE CUT ONE

SUNGLASSES CASE
PAGE 33

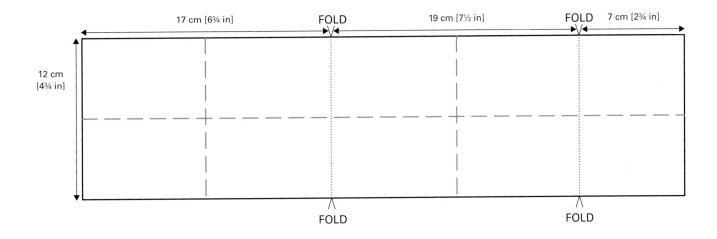

17 cm [6¾ in]   FOLD   19 cm [7½ in]   FOLD   7 cm [2¾ in]

12 cm [4¾ in]

FOLD   FOLD

BAG KEEPER
PAGE 32

The elephant and his bag can be squared up to any size you want. Embroidering the words is optional.

PEG BAG
PAGE 44

1 square = 2.5 cm [1 in]

A front cut one

B back cut one

C lining cut one

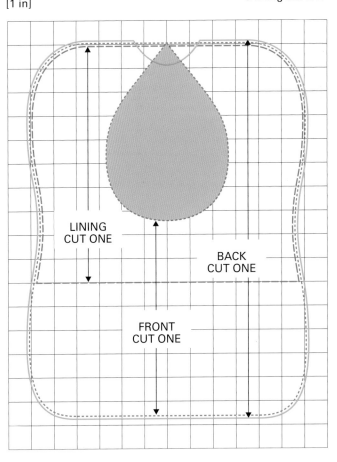

LINING CUT ONE

BACK CUT ONE

FRONT CUT ONE

NIGHTDRESS

PAGE 53

Enlarge the pattern shapes onto a large sheet of squared pattern paper. Pin the cut-out shapes to your fabric. Be sure to place both centre skirt sections on a fold.

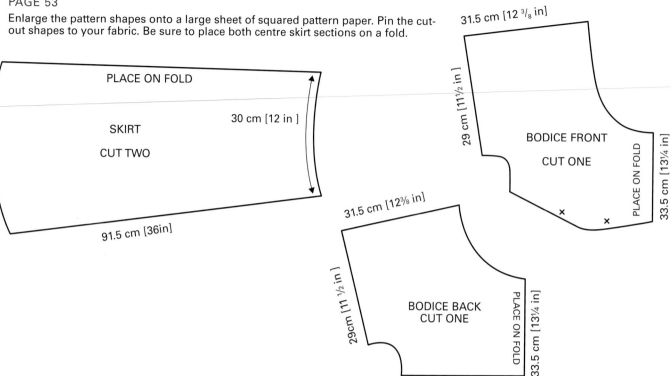

PLACE ON FOLD

SKIRT

CUT TWO

30 cm [12 in]

91.5 cm [36in]

31.5 cm [12 3/8 in]

29 cm [11½ in]

BODICE FRONT

CUT ONE

PLACE ON FOLD

33.5 cm [13¼ in]

31.5 cm [12⅜ in]

29cm [11 ½ in]

BODICE BACK
CUT ONE

PLACE ON FOLD

33.5 cm [13¼ in]

26.5 cm [10½ in]

CAMISOLE

PAGE 64

Each square = 2.3 cm [⅞ in] for 82 cm [32 in] bust
Alter square value for larger or smaller sizes.

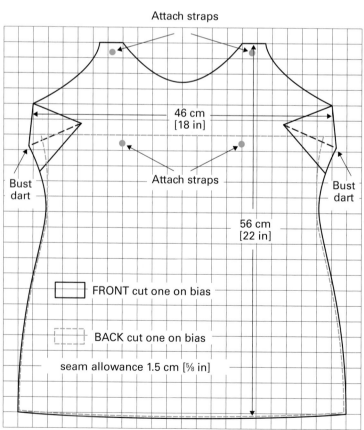

Attach straps

46 cm
[18 in]

Attach straps

Bust
dart

Bust
dart

56 cm
[22 in]

FRONT cut one on bias

BACK cut one on bias

seam allowance 1.5 cm [⅝ in]

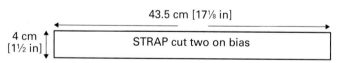

43.5 cm [17⅛ in]

4 cm
[1½ in]

STRAP cut two on bias

A-LINE SKIRT
PAGE 72

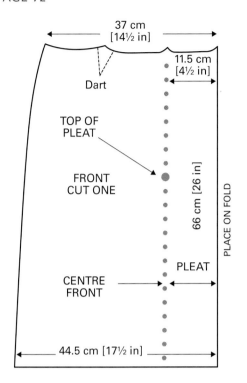

37 cm [14½ in]

Dart

11.5 cm [4½ in]

TOP OF PLEAT

FRONT CUT ONE

66 cm [26 in]

PLACE ON FOLD

CENTRE FRONT

PLEAT

44.5 cm [17½ in]

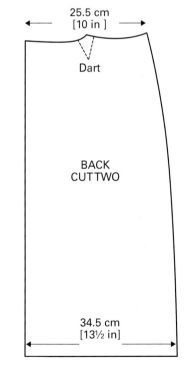

25.5 cm [10 in]

Dart

BACK CUT TWO

34.5 cm [13½ in]

PLACE ON FOLD

10.5 cm [4⅛ in]

WAISTBAND CUT ONE

44.5 cm [17½ in]

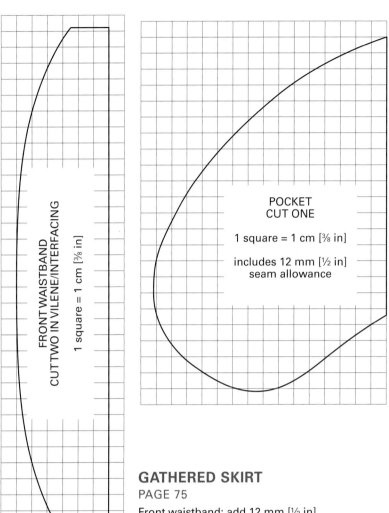

FRONT WAISTBAND
CUT TWO IN VILENE/INTERFACING

1 square = 1 cm [⅜ in]

POCKET CUT ONE

1 square = 1 cm [⅜ in]

includes 12 mm [½ in] seam allowance

GATHERED SKIRT
PAGE 75

Front waistband: add 12 mm [½ in] seam allowance all round and cut two in skirt fabric.

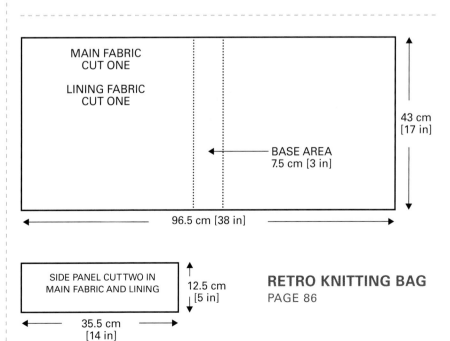

MAIN FABRIC CUT ONE

LINING FABRIC CUT ONE

BASE AREA 7.5 cm [3 in]

43 cm [17 in]

96.5 cm [38 in]

SIDE PANEL CUT TWO IN MAIN FABRIC AND LINING

12.5 cm [5 in]

35.5 cm [14 in]

RETRO KNITTING BAG
PAGE 86

APRON
PAGE 88

1 square = 38 mm [1½ in]

FOLD   FOLD

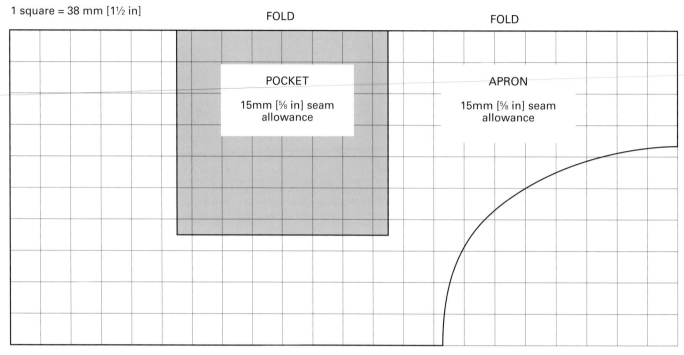

POCKET

15mm [⅝ in] seam
allowance

APRON

15mm [⅝ in] seam
allowance

PILLOWCASE WITH ENGLISH PATCHWORK ROSETTE
PAGE 94

Inner hexagon gives finished patch size and is also a template for papers. Enlarge or reduce via photocopier as desired.

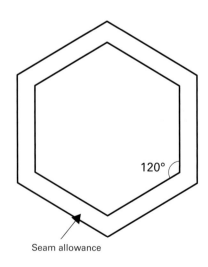

120°

Seam allowance

MULE SLIPPERS
PAGE 106

This slipper pattern will make up into UK women's shoe size 5–6 [US 7.5–8.5; EU 38–39]. Use a photocoper to gain the required measurements. Enlarge even further for men's sizes and reduce for children. The stars are matching points.

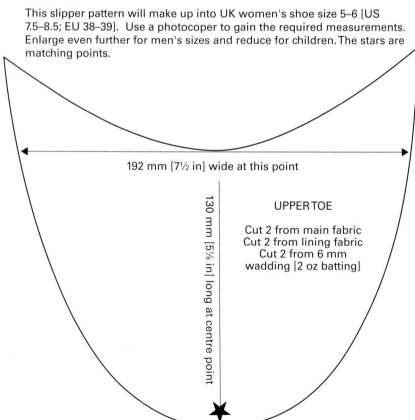

192 mm [7½ in] wide at this point

130 mm [5⅛ in] long at centre point

UPPER TOE

Cut 2 from main fabric
Cut 2 from lining fabric
Cut 2 from 6 mm
wadding [2 oz batting]

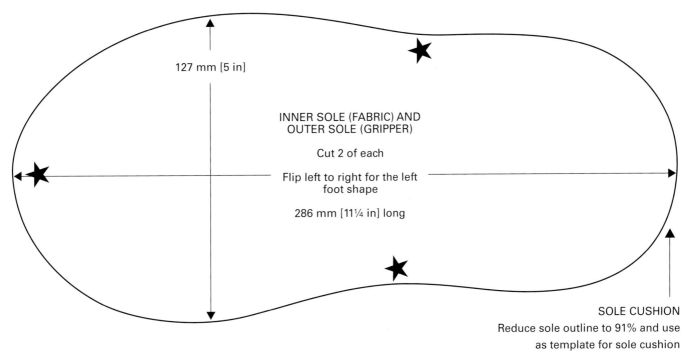

127 mm [5 in]

INNER SOLE (FABRIC) AND
OUTER SOLE (GRIPPER)

Cut 2 of each

Flip left to right for the left
foot shape

286 mm [11¼ in] long

SOLE CUSHION
Reduce sole outline to 91% and use
as template for sole cushion

Cut 2 from 25 mm wadding [6 oz batting]

Overall length = 260 mm [10¼ in]

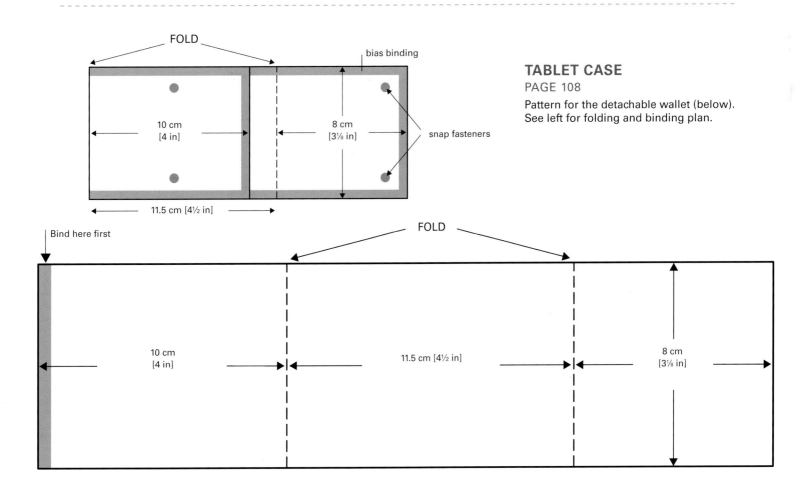

FOLD

bias binding

10 cm
[4 in]

8 cm
[3⅛ in]

snap fasteners

11.5 cm [4½ in]

TABLET CASE
PAGE 108
Pattern for the detachable wallet (below).
See left for folding and binding plan.

Bind here first

FOLD

10 cm
[4 in]

11.5 cm [4½ in]

8 cm
[3⅛ in]

XMAS STOCKING

PAGE 116

Each square = 38 mm [1½ in]

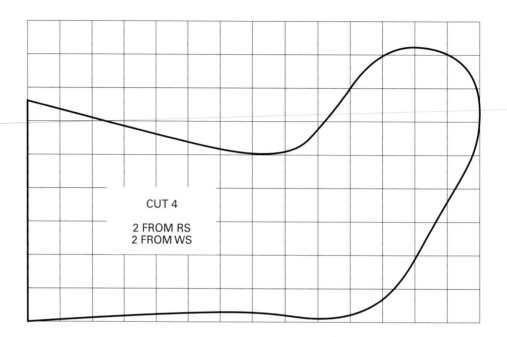

CUT 4

2 FROM RS
2 FROM WS

TEMPLATES FOR EGG COSIES

PAGE 90

These are same size templates so you can copy, scan or trace directly from the page.

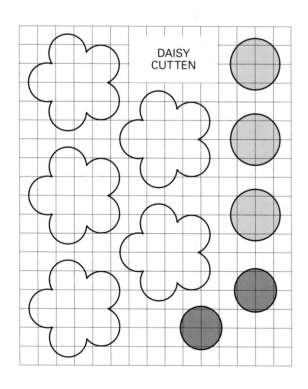

DAISY
CUT TEN

EGG COSIES

PAGE 90

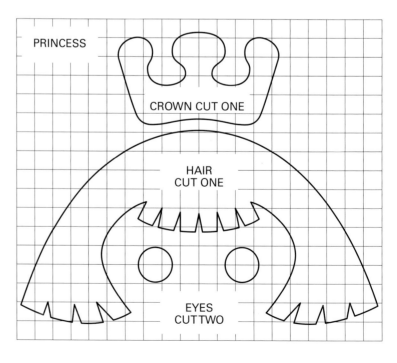

PRINCESS

CROWN CUT ONE

HAIR
CUT ONE

EYES
CUT TWO

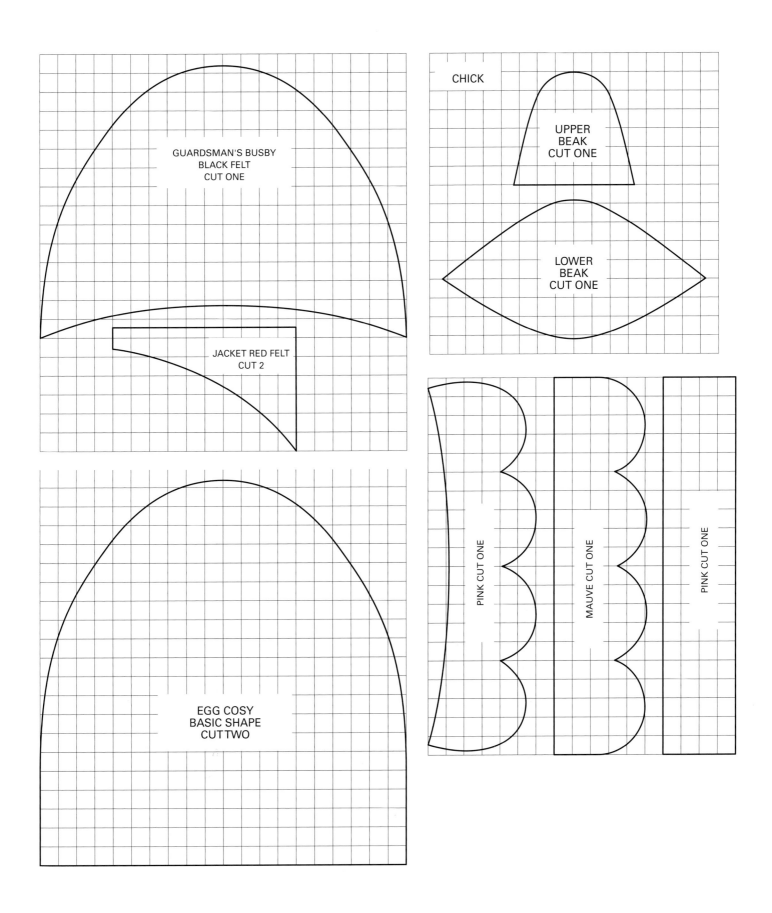

GUARDSMAN'S BUSBY
BLACK FELT
CUT ONE

JACKET RED FELT
CUT 2

EGG COSY
BASIC SHAPE
CUT TWO

CHICK

UPPER
BEAK
CUT ONE

LOWER
BEAK
CUT ONE

PINK CUT ONE

MAUVE CUT ONE

PINK CUT ONE

MENING

Grandmothers always used to say 'Never send a hole to the wash,' because the rigours of the wash tub and mangle would almost certainly make it larger. Nowadays, with 'delicate' cycles on our washing machines, little damage can be done by laundering our worn or torn things first. So prepare your mending by washing, drying, and trimming away any loose threads or raw edges.

USING STRAIGHT STITCHES

Running stitch and back stitch are those most commonly used for mending seams and casings (p. 14). Crossed seams – where four pieces of fabric are joined at the crotch or underarm of a garment – frequently need repair and to do this you will have to turn the garment inside out to replace the broken stitches. Begin and end 1 cm [½ in] either side of the break, where the stitching is still good. Where a line of top stitching has given way on a casing or on a flat fell seam (p. 39) you can easily mend that from the right side. Always secure the repair thread at start and finish with a back stitch; knots put unnecessary strain on threads and will show through fine fabric when ironed.

OVERSEWING

Used for sewing two neatened edges together, for example when mending a tear, or attaching a tie-belt or length of trim to a garment. First secure thread with two small stitches on the spot and carry on with neat diagonal stitches equally spaced. This stitch can be done from left to right or vice versa (p. 15).

OVERSEWING A BROKEN ZIP

Provided the teeth are missing near the bottom of the zip [zipper] it can be mended by pulling the slider above the break and oversewing a new stop across both rows of teeth. Use ordinary sewing cotton doubled. If it is a heavy-duty zip, you could oversew with something stronger, such as button thread.

SLIP STITCH

Used for stitching a folded edge invisibly to a flat surface (p. 15). Catch up a few threads of flat fabric with your needle, enter fold and slide along inside for up to 1 cm [½ in] before coming out again to make the next stitch.

REPAIRING A SLEEVE LINING

Slip stitch is ideal for repairing a sleeve lining at the cuff. If worn through, the lining can be completely undone around the inner cuff and turned up to hide the worn section. Pin the new fold and slip stitch the lining back into place.

DARNING AND PATCHING

Thanks to synthetic fibres, socks are rarely darned these days; and with mass production of inexpensive clothing, we're not so keen on patching garments either. The exception to the rule is likely to be a much-loved pair of jeans.

If you need to make a surface repair to a small tear in the denim, first stitch it together edge-to-edge before darning across the split. Extend the darn beyond the tear, into the undamaged area of denim.

A hole or large split can be patched, either on the surface or from the inside. Take a piece of un-worn denim or contrasting fabric for the repair. Cut it large enough to extend into the undamaged area. If the contrast fabric is lightweight, you could use fusible web to bond it to an extra layer for support.

Tack [baste] the patch either over or under the denim. Switch to the holed side and cut the raw edges right back before turning it under with running stitch that passes through the patch fabric as well.

Switch sides again and turn the patch edges under. Hem or herringbone stitch (p. 23) the patch to the denim leaving no raw edges inside or out. If you wish, embellish with decorative stitching using embroidery cotton [floss].

LAUNDRY AND AFTERCARE

LAUNDRY

Inspect the care symbols on any fabric that you buy; the manufacturer's care label appears on the bolt itself. Other points of reference are your own washing machine and tumble drier manuals. These contain details of all the washing and drying programs, indicating how they tie in with the standard care symbols.

If possible, deal quickly with stains. Don't rub the affected area because friction can disturb the fibres and leave an obvious patch. Oil-based marks should be treated from the wrong side of the fabric with a proper solvent, following manufacturer's instructions.

Whether hand or machine washing, do not use washing powder on fabrics with high wool or silk content, use soap flakes or liquid instead. The cleansing agents in liquid soaps are designed to work at low temperatures and won't leave a powdery deposit. Liquid soap works equally well on man-made fibres in hard water areas. Test strong colours (especially reds) for colourfastness and if in any doubt wash t hem separately.

Woollen fabrics should always be rinsed in warm water. Use the machine-washable wool setting on your machine, not the low-temperature or hand-wash program that delivers a cold rinse. Lift them from the washing machine with care and roll in a clean towel to remove excess water. Lay woollens and any jersey knit fabrics to dry flat on a drying rack. Do not line dry because they could lose shape as the moisture drains downward.

Iron fabrics according to the recommended heat setting. Take care with trimmings. Nylon lace, metallic threads and plastic sequins will shrivel at the touch of a hot iron.

'Pressing' is often used for 'ironing' but more strictly it means using steam and a pressing cloth. It is important to lift the iron straight up and down and not to pull it across the fabric when steam pressing.

AFTERCARE

It is worth investing in good quality hangers for the clothes that you make. Sew hanging loops inside shoulder seams and waistbands to make sure garments are properly supported, not drooping in deep folds from a distorted shoulder line. Evening dresses and other delicate fabrics should hang inside protective covers to keep them clear of the floor and free from too much handling.

When storing clothes and household linen, put items away clean, absolutely dry, and unstarched (the silverfish pest loves to eat starch). Dust, dirt and perspiration can harm and discolour fibres of all kinds – synthetics as well as natural – and both moths and moulds feed readily on dirt.

Precious heirlooms like christening and wedding gowns should be laundered or dry cleaned, then interleaved with plenty of acid-free tissue paper and stored in zipped cotton cases. Keep curtains, loose covers and bed quilts well-protected in chests and cupboards, or inside zipped covers and lidded plastic boxes for long-term storage. Shake them out occasionally and roll or refold a different way to prevent permanent creases from setting in.

Avoid mould or mildew by never storing fabrics in poorly ventilated, damp or humid surroundings such as lofts, cellars or seldom-opened cupboards. Low-powered heaters and dehumidifiers can help to reduce problems caused by damp and condensation.

Watch out for the tiny clothes moth. It has a life cycle of around six weeks, and its larvae chew ruinous holes in things. Nowadays, there are pleasantly scented alternatives to camphor mothballs, such as cedarwood blocks and lavender bags, although you should renew these occasionally. Moths not only lay their eggs on wool but can also attack silk, fur or feathers. It is a wise precaution to check your storage places every so often; keep disturbing the moths' potential habitat and they won't settle.

GLOSSARY OF SEWING TERMS

Armscye [US] The armhole of a garment

Appliqué The technique of stitching one fabric on top of another

Basting [Tacking] Temporary stitches made with running stitch about 1.5 cm [½ in] long

Bias Any diagonal line between lengthwise and crosswise grains. 'True' bias, at 45 degrees to the selvedge [selvage], gives maximum stretch

Bias binding Binding strip cut on the bias to fit smoothly around curves without adding bulk. Purchase readymade, or cut from the fabric in hand to make a 'self' bias binding

Binding A narrow strip of fabric or tape used to cover the raw edges of a garment. It can be hidden on the inside or sewn on the surface as decoration

Casing A tube of fabric designed to contain elastic, cord, ribbon etc

Dart A sewn structure that takes in fabric to give shape to a garment

Ease The adjustable difference between body measurement and paper pattern, especially used for setting sleeves in an armhole [armscye]

Facing Shaped piece of fabric (frequently interfaced) enclosing raw edges inside a sleeve or neck opening

Fusible web A synthetic material that bonds to fabric when melted by the heat of an iron

Gathers Small folds gathered by drawing up a line of stitching. Used to create frills [ruffles]

Grain line The direction in which the warp and weft threads lie. The warp running lengthwise, parallel to the selvedge, is the lengthwise grain. The weft follows the crosswise grain, at right angles to the selvedge

Hem The turned-up area at the bottom of a garment, which prevents fraying

Interfacing Extra fabric sewn or ironed between the layers of fabric to give it more body. Also called interlining

Lining A lightweight fabric (often taffeta or satin) sewn inside a garment to conceal seam allowances. Linings also block 'see-through' in a lightweight fabric

Nap Texture or design that runs in one direction only and influences pattern cutting layouts. 'With nap' fabrics include velvet, corduroy and satin

Notches Diamond-shaped marks that project beyond the pattern edge, for aligning pattern pieces at the sewing stage

Notions Incidental items such as thread, fastenings, tape and trimmings

Petersham Corded ribbon (similar to grosgrain) used to stiffen waistbands

Pile The soft raised surface on velvet, corduroy and some brushed fabrics. It usually has a nap that can affect the colour and influences pattern cutting layouts

Piping [Cording] Gives a neat firm finish to a seam, especially on soft furnishings. The cord should be pre-shrunk and encased in bias-cut strips

Pleat Folds controlling fabric fullness. Variations include box, inverted and knife pleats

Poppers [Snaps] Press stud fastenings

Pre-shrunk Fabric subjected to a shrinking process during manufacture

Pressing Often used for 'ironing' but more strictly means using steam and a pressing cloth

RS Abbreviation for 'Right Side'

Raw edge Untreated cut edge of a piece of fabric, which may fray or unravel

Rise Distance from crotch seam to waistband on trousers [pants]

Rouleau Narrow tubing constructed from bias strips, used for shoulder straps and applied decoration.

Seam Two pieces of fabric joined with a line of stitches. Variations include open, encased, French and flat fell seams

Seam allowance Distance between the cut edge and the seam line

Selvedge [Selvage] The solid edge of a woven fabric

Slip stitch Stitches that attach a folded edge virtually invisibly to a flat surface

Snap fasteners (Poppers) Press stud fastenings

Stay stitching A line of straight stitches that prevents curved or bias edges, such as necklines, shoulders and waistlines, from stretching out of shape during sewing

Tacking [Basting] Temporary stitches made with running stitch about 1.5 cm [½ in] long

Tailor's tacks Temporary loops of thread for matching points or marking the position of darts or pockets

Top stitching An extra row of stitching (usually decorative) done in matching or contrasting thread along or near a finished edge

WS Abbreviation for 'Wrong Side'

Warp Runs lengthwise, parallel to the selvedge [selvage], usually stronger than the weft

Weft Runs at right angles to the selvedge [selvage], not usually quite as strong as the warp